j
B
DRAKE, F.

17 × 7/09

P9-CJZ-910

B

WITHDRAWN

Sir Francis Drake
and the Struggle for an Ocean Empire

General Editor

William H. Goetzmann
Jack S. Blanton, Sr., Chair in History
   University of Texas at Austin

Consulting Editor

Tom D. Crouch
Chairman, Department of Aeronautics
   National Air and Space Museum
   Smithsonian Institution

WORLD EXPLORERS

Sir Francis Drake
and the Struggle for an Ocean Empire

Alice Smith Duncan

Introductory Essay by Michael Collins

CHELSEA HOUSE PUBLISHERS

New York   Philadelphia

On the cover Map of the world; portrait of Sir Francis Drake

Chelsea House Publishers
Editor-in-Chief Richard S. Papale
Executive Managing Editor Karyn Gullen Browne
Copy Chief Philip Koslow
Picture Editor Adrian G. Allen
Art Director Nora Wertz
Manufacturing Director Gerald Levine
Systems Manager Lindsey Ottman
Production Coordinator Marie Claire Cebrián-Ume

World Explorers
Senior Editor Sean Dolan

Staff for SIR FRANCIS DRAKE AND THE STRUGGLE FOR AN OCEAN EMPIRE
Copy Editor David Carter
Editorial Assistant Robert Kimball Green
Picture Researcher Wendy P. Wills
Senior Designer Basia Niemczyc

First printing

1 3 5 7 9 8 6 4 2

Library of Congress Cataloging-in-Publication Data

Duncan, Alice Smith
Sir Francis Drake and the struggle for an ocean empire / Alice Smith Duncan; introductory essay by Michael Collins.
    p. cm.—(World Explorers)
Includes bibliographical references and index.
Summary: Surveys the life and voyages of Sir Francis Drake and the expansion of the English naval fleet in the sixteenth century.
ISBN 0-7910-1302-2
    0-7910-1525-4 (pbk.)
1. Drake, Francis, Sir, 1540?–1596—Juvenile literature. 2. Great Britain—History, Naval—Tudors, 1485–1603—Juvenile literature. 3. America—Discovery and exploration—English—Juvenile literature. 4. Admirals—Great Britain—Biography—Juvenile literature. 5. Explorers—America—Biography—Juvenile literature. [1. Drake, Francis, Sir, 1540?–1596. 2. Admirals. 3. Explorers. 4. Great Britain—History, Naval—Tudors, 1485–1603.] I. Title. II. Series.   92-14271
DA86.22.D7D86 1993   CIP
942.05'5'092—dc20   AC
[B]

CONTENTS

WORLD EXPLORERS

THE EARLY EXPLORERS

Herodotus and the Explorers of the Classical Age
Marco Polo and the Medieval Explorers
The Viking Explorers

THE FIRST GREAT AGE OF DISCOVERY

Jacques Cartier, Samuel de Champlain, and the Explorers of Canada
Christopher Columbus and the First Voyages to the New World
From Coronado to Escalante: The Explorers of the Spanish Southwest
Hernando de Soto and the Explorers of the American South
Sir Francis Drake and the Struggle for an Ocean Empire
Vasco da Gama and the Portuguese Explorers
La Salle and the Explorers of the Mississippi
Ferdinand Magellan and the Discovery of the World Ocean
Pizarro, Orellana, and the Exploration of the Amazon
The Search for the Northwest Passage

THE SECOND GREAT AGE OF DISCOVERY

Roald Amundsen and the Quest for the South Pole
Daniel Boone and the Opening of the Ohio Country
Captain James Cook and the Explorers of the Pacific
The Explorers of Alaska
John Charles Frémont and the Great Western Reconnaissance
Alexander von Humboldt, Colossus of Exploration
Lewis and Clark and the Route to the Pacific
Alexander Mackenzie and the Explorers of Canada
Robert Peary and the Quest for the North Pole
Zebulon Pike and the Explorers of the American Southwest
John Wesley Powell and the Great Surveys of the American West
Jedediah Smith and the Mountain Men of the American West
Henry Stanley and the European Explorers of Africa
Lt. Charles Wilkes and the Great U.S. Exploring Expedition

THE THIRD GREAT AGE OF DISCOVERY

Apollo to the Moon
The Explorers of the Undersea World
The First Men in Space
The Mission to Mars and Beyond
Probing Deep Space

CHELSEA HOUSE PUBLISHERS

Into the Unknown

Michael Collins

It is difficult to define most eras in history with any precision, but not so the space age. On October 4, 1957, it burst on us with little warning when the Soviet Union launched *Sputnik*, a 184-pound cannonball that circled the globe once every 96 minutes. Less than 4 years later, the Soviets followed this first primitive satellite with the flight of Yuri Gagarin, a 27-year-old fighter pilot who became the first human to orbit the earth. The Soviet Union's success prompted President John F. Kennedy to decide that the United States should "land a man on the moon and return him safely to earth" before the end of the 1960s. We now had not only a space age but a space race.

I was born in 1930, exactly the right time to allow me to participate in Project Apollo, as the U.S. lunar program came to be known. As a young man growing up, I often found myself too young to do the things I wanted—or suddenly too old, as if someone had turned a switch at midnight. But for Apollo, 1930 was the perfect year to be born, and I was very lucky. In 1966 I enjoyed circling the earth for three days, and in 1969 I flew to the moon and laughed at the sight of the tiny earth, which I could cover with my thumbnail.

How the early explorers would have loved the view from space! With one glance Christopher Columbus could have plotted his course and reassured his crew that the world was indeed round. In 90 minutes Magellan could have looked down at every port of call in the *Victoria's* three-year circumnavigation of the globe. Given a chance to map their route from orbit, Lewis and Clark could have told President Jefferson that there was no easy Northwest Passage but that a continent of exquisite diversity awaited their scrutiny.

In a physical sense, we have already gone to most places that we can. That is not to say that there are not new adventures awaiting us in the sea or on the red plains of Mars, but more important than reaching new places will be understanding those we have already visited. There are vital gaps in our understanding of how our planet works as an ecosystem and how our planet fits into the infinite order of the universe. The next great age may well be the age of assimilation, in which we use microscope and telescope to evaluate what we have discovered and put that knowledge to use. The adventure of being first to reach may be replaced by the satisfaction of being first to grasp. Surely that is a form of exploration as vital to our well-being, and perhaps even survival, as the distinction of being the first to explore a specific geographical area.

The explorers whose stories are told in the books of this series did not just sail perilous seas, scale rugged mountains, traverse blistering deserts, dive to the depths of the ocean, or land on the moon. Their voyages and expeditions were journeys of mind as much as of time and distance, through which they—and all of mankind—were able to reach a greater understanding of our universe. That challenge remains, for all of us. The imperative is to see, to understand, to develop knowledge that others can use, to help nurture this planet that sustains us all. Perhaps being born in 1975 will be as lucky for a new generation of explorer as being born in 1930 was for Neil Armstrong, Buzz Aldrin, and Mike Collins.

The Reader's Journey

William H. Goetzmann

This volume is one of a series that takes us with the great explorers of the ages on bold journeys over the oceans and the continents and into outer space. As we travel along with these imaginative and creative journeyers, we share their adventures and their knowledge. We also get a glimpse of that mysterious and inextinguishable fire that burned in the breast of men such as Magellan and Columbus—the fire that has propelled all those throughout the ages who have been driven to leave behind family and friends for a voyage into the unknown.

No one has satisfactorily explained the urge to explore, the drive to go to the "back of beyond." It is certain that it has been present in man almost since he began walking erect and first ventured across the African savannas. Sparks from that same fire fueled the transoceanic explorers of the Ice Age, who led their people across the vast plain that formed a land bridge between Asia and North America, and the astronauts and scientists who determined that man must reach the moon.

Besides an element of adventure, all exploration involves an element of mystery. We must not confuse exploration with discovery. Exploration is a purposeful human activity—a search for something. Discovery may be the end result of that search; it may also be an accident, as when Columbus found a whole new world while searching for the Indies. Often, the explorer may not even realize the full significance of what he has discovered, as was the case with Columbus. Exploration, on the other hand, is the product of a cultural or individual curiosity; it is a unique process that has enabled mankind to know and understand the world's oceans, continents, and polar regions. It is at the heart of scientific thinking. One of its most significant aspects is that it teaches people to ask the right questions; by doing so, it forces us to reevaluate what we think we know and understand. Thus knowledge progresses, and we are driven constantly to a new awareness and appreciation of the universe in all its infinite variety.

The motivation for exploration is not always pure. In his fascination with the new, man often forgets that others have been there before him. For example, the popular notion of the discovery of America overlooks the complex Indian civilizations that had existed there for thousands of years before the arrival of Europeans. Man's desire for conquest, riches, and fame is often linked inextricably with his quest for the unknown, but a story that touches so closely on the human essence must of necessity treat war as well as peace, avarice with generosity, both pride and humility, frailty and greatness. The story of exploration is above all a story of humanity and of man's understanding of his place in the universe.

The WORLD EXPLORERS series has been divided into four sections. The first treats the explorers of the ancient world, the Viking explorers of the 9th through the 11th centuries, and Marco Polo and the medieval explorers. The rest of the series is divided into three great ages of exploration. The first is the era of Columbus and Magellan: the period spanning the 15th and 16th centuries, which saw the discovery and exploration of the New World and the world ocean. The second might be called the age of science and imperialism, the era made possible by the scientific advances of the 17th century, which witnessed the discovery of the world's last two undiscovered continents, Australia and Antarctica, the mapping of all the continents and oceans, and the establishment of colonies all over the world. The third great age refers to the most ambitious quests of the 20th century—the probing of space and of the ocean's depths.

As we reach out into the darkness of outer space and other galaxies, we come to better understand how our ancestors confronted *oecumene,* or the vast earthly unknown. We learn once again the meaning of an unknown 18th-century sea captain's advice to navigators:

> And if by chance you make a landfall on the shores of another sea in a far country inhabited by savages and barbarians, remember you this: the greatest danger and the surest hope lies not with fires and arrows but in the quicksilver hearts of men.

At its core, exploration is a series of moral dramas. But it is these dramas, involving new lands, new people, and exotic ecosystems of staggering beauty, that make the explorers' stories not only moral tales but also some of the greatest adventure stories ever recorded. They represent the process of learning in its most expansive and vivid forms. We see that real life, past and present, transcends even the adventures of the starship *Enterprise.*

FRANCISCVS DRAECK NOBILISSIMVS EQVES ANGLIÆ ANⁿ ÆT SVE 43

Habes Lector candide sortiß, ac inuictuß Ducis Draeck ad viuum Imaginem qui
toto terrarum orbe, duorum annorum, et mensum decem spatio, Zephiris fauen:
tibus circumducto, Angliam sedes proprias, 4. Cal Octobr, anno à partu Virgi:
nis 1580 reuisit cum antea portu soluißet Id. Decem: anni 1577.

The Master Thief of the Unknown World

On a brisk incoming tide on the afternoon of September 26, 1580, a weather-beaten ship—the *Golden Hind*—sailed up the English Channel toward the port city of Plymouth. The tattered members of its crew cheered each landmark it passed—the Scilly Isles, Wolf Rock, the stony promontory called the Lizard—for they were at last in home waters, and over the course of their long voyage they had often doubted they would see these familiar sights again.

The captain, Francis Drake, peered apprehensively toward the harbor entrance ahead. At the mouth of Plymouth Sound he drew his heavily laden ship close by a small fishing boat and hailed the startled fishermen. The scent of exotic spices from the ship's hold perfumed the sea breeze as Drake, leaning over the high deck railing, shouted down an urgent question: "Is the Queen still alive?"

With the fishermen's positive reply, Drake relaxed slightly, and in a short time the ship rounded the last point and brought up at safe anchorage in its busy home port. "We had spent," wrote an anonymous member of the crew, "2 years, 10 months and some few odd days beside, in seeing the wonders of the Lord in the deep, in discovering so many admirable things, in going through with so many strange adventures, in escaping out of so many dangers and overcoming so many difficulties in this our encompassing of this nether globe."

Sir Francis Drake, after an engraving made by the Dutch artist Jodocus Hondius following the English mariner's successful circumnavigation of the world. According to the historian John Sugden, Drake "was not more than medium in height, possibly even short, but he was thick-set, robust and powerful, with broad shoulders and strong limbs. His head was round, with a high forehead, and his eyes large, open and bright, lending his face the 'merry' aspect that accorded with his demeanour."

An artist's conception of the
Golden Hind, *which carried
Drake and 58 of his men around
the world. Though it is in all likelihood the most famous ship in
English maritime history, there
are no surviving contemporary
descriptions of the precise dimen-
sions of the* Golden Hind. *It was
probably no more than 70 feet
long and 20 feet wide, with built-
up cabin and cargo sections—
called castles—at the bow and
the stern.*

Almost three years before, Drake had left Plymouth in
command of the best-equipped naval expedition ever
launched by England: five stout ships, well armed and
well provisioned, crewed by more than 150 men, most of
them seasoned mariners but including as well an artist, a
band of musicians, and a group of inexperienced young
aristocrats in search of adventure. He returned with a single
ship and a half-starved crew of 58 that had not set foot on
a populated shore for six months.

Not a word of news from home had reached them during
their journey, which had taken them around the world
through waters either hostile or uncharted. The hold of
their sturdy little ship carried the richest cargo ever to
have reached an English port—tons of spices and precious metals, jewels, silks, fine porcelains, and irreplaceable
maps—yet still Drake hesitated to assume they would be

welcomed, for his actions in obtaining the material tokens of his voyage's success made him little better than a pirate. He alone knew that Queen Elizabeth herself had approved any means, piracy included, to assure the expedition's profitable outcome, but he had sworn his oath to keep her involvement secret; if she now was no longer in a position to acknowledge and defend him, Drake understood, he might pay for his triumph with his head.

So he insisted his crew endure one more hardship before reuniting with their friends and families. While the others waited impatiently on board the *Golden Hind*, a few men went ashore in a small boat with instructions to bring back the captain's wife, Mary, from Drake's harborside home. She brought with her the mayor of Plymouth, and in the privacy of his cabin, as the crew waited on deck yearning to disembark, Drake learned that enemies and friends alike had for months posted lookouts in every Channel harbor, watching for his return. Although he still had supporters in Elizabeth's court, much had happened in his absence and the political situation was extremely delicate. He was advised to send secret word of his arrival to London and to hide out of public view while awaiting further instructions from the queen or his supporters at court. Moreover, the mayor informed him, Plymouth was in the grip of an epidemic of the plague.

This last was the excuse Drake offered his frustrated crew as he had the mayor and Mary set ashore and ordered the ship ready to put back out into the Channel. After dispatches announcing his return were sent to the queen and three members of her Privy Council, the *Golden Hind* slipped away from Plymouth toward a deserted Channel island (now known as Drake's Island). There, at the mercy of shifting political winds as furious as anything they had weathered at sea, captain and crew spent several anxious days.

When Drake's expedition left England in 1577, not even the crew knew its real destination until long after it left

European waters. Though it had the backing of many of the nation's most powerful individuals, many of these were silent partners, and its objectives were cloaked in secrecy for fear of provoking war with Spain, overlord of the richest and largest empire on the globe.

In the approximately 150 years preceding Drake's voyage, Portugal and then Spain had made themselves the dominant powers in Europe by the "discovery" and then conquest of overseas colonies. Portugal established forts and trading outposts on both of Africa's coasts and, after pioneering a new sea route there around the Cape of Good Hope, in the Indies. Spain, in the wake of Christopher Columbus's famous voyages for Ferdinand and Isabella, controlled fabulously wealthy colonies in the Antilles (the islands of the Caribbean) and on the mainlands of North and South America.

Columbus's discovery of the New World precipitated a dispute between the two Iberian nations. Each wished to protect its sea routes—Portugal, the eastern route to the Indies around Africa's southern tip; Spain, the western route to the lands discovered by Columbus—from the other and from foreign interlopers, so they agreed to submit the thorny question of jurisdiction to the pope, whose authority, in those years before the Protestant Reformation, was acknowledged by all of Christian Europe.

Pope Alexander VI's solution, ratified in the Treaty of Tordesillas, was simple. A theoretical line was drawn north to south through the Atlantic Ocean about 2,300 miles west of the Cape Verde Islands. All non-Christian lands to the east were Portugal's; those to the west were Spain's.

By the mid-1500s, gold and silver from the New World and slaves, silks, and spices from Africa and the Orient had made Spain and Portugal the richest nations in Europe, and the Iberian nations grew ever more determined to guard their monopolies. By 1570, Spain was rigidly enforcing a policy of refusing to permit any foreign nation to engage in commercial trade with its New World colonies.

But the pope's rulings and Spain's determination could not completely deter competition from the seafaring powers of Europe that were thereby theoretically excluded from commerce with the Orient and the New World, especially once the effects of the Reformation had lessened the spiritual and temporal authority of the pope and made religious enemies of nations that had previously shared an adherence to Roman Catholicism. Investors in England, as well as in France and the Netherlands, surreptitiously outfitted expeditions for the purpose of plundering Spanish shipping in the English Channel and along the coasts of the Spanish Main. In time, these marauding captains, known as corsairs or privateers, also became instruments of foreign policy, used consciously by their governments to strike at the Spanish empire. Like Drake, many regarded their buccaneering more as a highly profitable form of patriotism than as piracy.

Drake's recently concluded voyage, in which he had circumnavigated the globe, was the most notorious privateering exploit of the Elizabethan Age. After relieving Spanish ships and ports of their treasures up and down the west coast of South America, he set off across the Pacific and Indian oceans. In flagrant disregard of Portugal's ordained trade monopoly over the Indies, he then proceeded to negotiate commercial rights for precious spices with island rulers along his escape route. As he guided the *Golden Hind* through the Orient, Drake had no way of knowing that the king of Portugal lay dying. Nor, before he made his wary return to England, could he have known that just three months earlier, Spain had overrun Portugal and claimed all its territories: his offenses against Portugal were now added to the sum of his transgressions against Spain.

His swashbuckling presented Elizabeth with a dilemma. The queen had intended that Drake's mission annoy Spain's king, Philip II—"to singe his beard," as Drake would later say about an even more daring escapade—but she had in all likelihood never imagined that his

This silver cup was just one of many gifts given by Queen Elizabeth to Drake in recognition of his service to the realm. It was originally intended to encase a coconut that Drake had brought back with him from his circumnavigation and presented to the queen as a sample of the strange things he had seen in the course of his epic voyage.

provocation would prove so outrageous. England was small, isolated, militarily weak, and relatively poor, an island nation torn by conflict between Catholics and Protestants; militantly Catholic Spain controlled the largest and richest empire that history had yet produced.

The risks attached to provoking Spain too far were obvious. Though he received a warning from well-placed friends that the queen was displeased with him, as the Spanish ambassador was demanding restitution for the robberies he had committed, Drake's penchant for daredeviltry left him willing to gamble that his loot would buy him favor at court. In his message to London, Drake had described his cargo in the most tempting terms, and he knew his expedition's backers could not fail to be impressed by a promised return on their investment of almost 5,000 percent. Four days later, official word arrived. Elizabeth summoned Drake to her court, assuring him that as of yet he had nothing to fear and of her great interest in seeing some of the "curiosities" he had gathered on his way around the world.

Drake had met his queen just once, during the preparations for the voyage, but that experience had been sufficient to impress him with her high mettle, her shrewd character, her ambitious intelligence, and her keen appraisal of the economic realities confronting her struggling realm. He had noted as well her love of display and her spirited admiration of boldness. He therefore interpreted her summons as an opportunity to demonstrate the actual richness of the ends accomplished by his politically unfortunate means. He made ready a cavalcade of pack horses laden with gold, silver, fabrics, and all his treasure trove's most fascinating and exotic examples of jewelry, including a crown set with emeralds and a diamond-encrusted frog that he would later give to the queen as a gift.

The queen granted the flamboyant buccaneer a private, six-hour audience in which to display his opulent pelf. The great stateswoman listened spellbound to her scapegrace captain elaborate on the tales and details of his journey as, opening chest after chest, he poured out cascades of treasure at her feet. The new knowledge he imparted to her poured forth in equally prodigious abundance. He presented her with the only copy of the diary he had kept of the journey's key events; this priceless volume, since lost, was filled with meticulous paintings and drawings he and the expedition's artist had made of new lands, cultures, and creatures discovered in her name. She heard for the first time of the Doldrums, a vast, maddening, windless stretch of the equatorial Atlantic, and of the treacherous shoals that lurked beneath the crosscurrents of the Strait of Magellan. He told her of encountering raging storms on the "peaceful" Pacific that separated him forever from the rest of his fleet and drove him against his will ever farther south but thereby enabled him to discover that the Atlantic and Pacific oceans join below the tip of South America—precisely where Europe's leading geographers and cartographers had insistently predicted a new continent must lie.

This discovery, Elizabeth understood, potentially opened an unimpeded route for other English ships (Spain claiming control over the Strait itself) to follow to the western American coasts Drake described to her next. By sailing North America's coastal waters northward as far as 48 degrees north latitude (near the location of present-day Vancouver, Canada) without coming upon the so-called Strait of Anian, the water passage that supposedly coursed northeast across the continent to the Atlantic, Drake had proved all contemporary beliefs about North American geography wrong.

Though that particular demonstration of the mistaken notions of her cosmographers may well have disappointed the queen's expectations—such a passage would have been of inestimable economic and strategic value—her enthusiasm revived upon learning that Drake had laid claim in her name to a vast and beautiful land that he

Queen Elizabeth I ruled England from 1558 to 1603, a period that, despite the constant external threat posed by Spain, has since come to be regarded as a golden age. During her reign, England advanced from a relatively isolated island nation to a genuine European power, negated Spain's attempts to extend its influence, developed a powerful navy, claimed its first overseas colonies, and experienced a flowering of the arts.

called Nova Albion (present-day California). His recounting of his subsequent negotiations with the sultan of Ternate, ruler of some of the most important Spice Islands in the Portuguese-claimed East Indies, whereby he obtained trading privileges in exchange for a commitment to help the islanders oust the Portuguese, also found favor with his royal listener. That Drake's lone ship had capped these adventures and accomplishments with a safe, almost nonstop six-month sea voyage home demonstrated to his queen that he was a mariner without equal and that naval ability and daring might win England a place in world commerce in spite of Spain's vast advantages.

Elizabeth was thrilled, but torn. Her secret delight in Drake's derring-do and her certainty that he was a man that England could rally around—his earlier privateering exploits had already inspired the composition of laudatory ballads and pamphlets—was tempered by her concern about Spain's reaction. Her counselors believed that open support for Drake would intolerably strain the patience of Philip, whose ambassador, Bernardino de Mendoza, was threatening in the king's name everything from reprisals against the English merchant community to outright war if the stolen treasure was not returned.

Torn between her desire for peace, her need for cash, and her private enthusiasm for Drake's exploits, Elizabeth decided on a shrewd scheme. She informed Mendoza that an examination of her captain's conduct had convinced her that he was innocent of damaging Spanish property and that ownership of the valuables would be determined in the civil courts, an uncertain process sure to take months. In the meantime, she decreed, the treasure would be inventoried in Plymouth and then stored in the Tower of London. But Drake, the queen's representatives, and his sponsors were granted secret access to the treasure before the inventory—only 5 of the original 26 tons of silver and a chest or two of gold and jewels ever reached the Tower.

The bluff worked. By January 1581, Philip had not protested further, and Elizabeth was sufficiently emboldened to announce that she intended to visit the *Golden Hind* in the spring. To Mendoza's outrage, Drake had become the court favorite and was spending much time in the company of the queen, whose admiring preference for the companionship of this boldly swaggering sailor she called her "sea-dog"—a commoner, no less—infuriated many of her foppish, well-born courtiers as well.

The crisis with Spain no longer seemed to frighten Elizabeth. She challenged Philip even further by renewing her marriage negotiations with Francis, duke of Alençon and Anjou, the younger brother of King Henri III of France. The prospective match hinged on politics, not love; Francis, like Elizabeth, was a Protestant, and he was an impor-

The dominant strains in the character of King Philip II of Spain were his devotion to duty—"Being a king is nothing but a kind of slavery that carries a crown," he once wrote—and his militant Catholicism. Reserved and prone to self-doubt, he ruled his far-flung empire from a desk in a spartan cell in the library of the Escorial, the massive, gloomy palace and monastery he built in the mountains near Madrid. Though some regarded his attention to every bureaucratic detail of his empire's administration as insufficiently kingly—Philip was "the best of his secretaries," a contemporary gibed—under his rule Spain expanded its foreign dominions to their greatest extent.

tant ally to the embattled Protestant leaders of the Netherlands, which was then engaged in a desperate struggle to
obtain its independence from Catholic Spain. Philip, who
was himself a spurned suitor of Elizabeth, had long feared
an alliance between England and France.

But the clearest demonstration of Elizabeth's boldness was
the visit she paid to the *Golden Hind* in April. Drake was
now the toast of his countrymen. They "generally ap-
plauded his wonderful long adventures and rich prizes,"
wrote a contemporary chronicler; "his name and fame
became admirable in all places, the people swarming daily
in the streets to behold him, vowing hatred to all that
misliked him." Yet all their praises could not compare to
the honor, for this common-born hero, of a royal visit.

For months, Drake devoted himself to the preparations
for what Mendoza seethingly described in a report to Philip
as the most sumptuous banquet seen in England since the
days of Elizabeth's father, the flamboyant Henry VIII. Casks
of the finest wines were ordered; chefs trained in the
making of exotic sauces prepared sample dishes featuring
seafood, meats, and game flavored with saffron and am-
bergris to be served on plates of silver and gold; the most
skillful masquers, musicians, and jugglers were hired; and a
wardrobe of special finery for Drake's family and household
servants was tailored for the occasion.

The *Golden Hind* was brought up the Thames River
toward London and fitted out like a pageant ship. Banners
emblazoned with the royal coat of arms, sewn in gold on
silk damask, were raised on masts and spars along with silk
streamers that billowed down to the water, and thickly
embroidered tapestries hung from the rigging on all decks.
The queen arrived with her full retinue on April 4. Tall and
slender, her face and bearing regally imperious, she stood
on the small ship's cramped afterdeck following the feasting
and her tour of the vessel, her jewel-studded gown glisten-
ing in the long plays of the afternoon's light, and raised a

golden sword high above the bent neck of Drake, who had knelt his burly form before her.

"My royal brother, the King of Spain, has demanded your head," she announced. The hushed crowd of courtiers gasped and pressed closer. They stared in confusion and delight as the queen then handed the sword to Alençon's proxy, who stood at her side, and said with a smile, "We shall ask Monsieur to be the headsman."

Instead, the French nobleman performed chivalry's most ancient rite of honor. Tapping gently once and again with the ceremonial blade at the shoulders of the kneeling seaman, he pronounced Drake a knight of the realm and bid him, "Arise, Sir Knight, the master thief of the unknown world."

In this romanticized conception of Drake's knighting on April 4, 1581, Queen Elizabeth herself, rather than a diplomat from France, wields the blade. The knighting was a bold stroke, for even though outright hostilities did not commence for several years, it was tantamount to a declaration of war by England against Spain.

The Education
of a Sea Dog

Francis Drake was born in 1541 in a rustic cottage on a nobleman's estate in the West Country of England near Tavistock, some 20 miles north of the famous seaport of Plymouth. He was the oldest of 12 sons. His father, Edmund Drake, was an ardent Protestant farmer who had probably been a sailor before the birth of his boys. Protestantism was common among English seamen at that time, possibly because their seafaring often brought them to northern Europe, where the Protestant Reformation was born in the second decade of the 16th century, but in the rural West Country Roman Catholics were still in the majority. In 1549, during the brief reign of the young Protestant king, Edward VI, they rose in rebellion when the monarch decreed that a prayerbook written in English, rather than Latin—the language of worship in the Catholic church—should be used throughout the country.

The Drake family was among those forced to flee from the violence in order to preserve their lives, and they lost the little property they possessed. This experience marked the beginning of Francis Drake's lifelong, often irrational hatred of Catholicism, which was nurtured by the outspoken anger of his parents and their fellow refugees.

Their flight took the Drakes more than a hundred miles to Chatham, a town southeast of London that was the site of the royal dockyard established a decade earlier by King Henry VIII as part of his efforts to build an English navy. The Drakes, nearly penniless but resourceful, made

A Spanish map of the Americas, dated 1562. "We Spanish suffer from a disease of the heart which can be cured only by gold," wrote Hernán Cortés, conqueror of the powerful Aztec empire in Mexico, and it seemed for a time that in the Americas he and his like-minded countrymen—the conquistadores—had found their panacea. The gold and silver that Spain extracted from the New World enabled Philip II to carry out what has been described as the most ambitious foreign policy since ancient Rome's.

a home for themselves there in the hulk of an abandoned warship that lay beached on the banks of the River Medway.

Edmund Drake, a literate man and a "hot gospeler" of his faith, was appointed as preacher and Bible reader to Chatham's seamen and shipwrights, most of whom could not read for themselves. His father's Bible was probably the source of much of Francis's education as well, for he learned to read and write as a child without ever attending school. The rest of his early learning came from his exposure to the sailors who were constantly shipping in and out of Chatham. It was a time, according to a contemporary, when "nothing was talked of among the mercantile or adventurous part of mankind but the beauty and riches of [the] new world. Fresh discoveries were frequently made, new countries and nations, never heard of before, were daily described." From their tales Francis learned also of the fabled serpents and innumerable superstitions of the sea and of the gruesome doings of the Spanish Inquisition. The terrors of the Inquisition, which had been established by Ferdinand and Isabella to root out heresy, were then very much a concern of English mariners, for it was well known that Protestants who fell into Spanish hands were often tortured to death.

It is not difficult to understand why Francis and many of his brothers went to sea. As the tides lifted and shifted the groaning boards of their makeshift home, masts and rigging, guns, cleats, and cannons, and billowing sails filled their every vista. The banging of hammers and scraping of carpenters' planes against hardwood carried clearly from the dockyard, and the sea chanties sung by the mariners as they polished the brightwork and swabbed down the decks provided the Drake children with their play songs and lullabies alike.

Edward VI was succeeded on the throne in 1553 by Queen Mary, a devout Catholic soon known as Bloody Mary because of her violent determination to restore Catholicism in England. Protestants who resisted her will were hanged; their swinging corpses were a common sight on the street corners of London and along the banks of the Medway. Though he escaped the gallows, Edmund Drake lost his job and was forced soon afterward to apprentice 12-year-old Francis to the owner of a small cargo boat.

Though apprenticeship was often an exceedingly unpleasant experience for a young lad, Drake had not been committed to a cruel master, simply to a harsh career. His master hauled coal and timber across the English Channel to France and the Netherlands in a small sailing ship; he may also, once Elizabeth succeeded Edward on the throne in 1558, have smuggled French and Dutch Protestants to safety in England. Drake apparently was an adept student and a hard worker who learned quickly the intricacies of piloting a cumbersome, overladen ship through all kinds of conditions by following landmarks and his instincts, for when the master died, probably around 1560, he bequeathed his ship to his apprentice.

Though the Channel trade was lucrative enough to provide Drake with a comfortable living, he tired of it quickly and sold his ship. Already, his essential character was well defined: The short, stocky, strongly built young man "of a cheerful countenance" lit by large, piercing blue eyes and topped with reddish brown hair was ambitious, bold, some would say greedy, and eager for adventure.

Drake returned to Plymouth, where his father had distant cousins named Hawkins, a very rich family of merchant shipowners. William Hawkins had been naval adviser to Henry VIII and had made the first English voyages to Brazil; his son John, between 1562 and 1565, made his own reputation in the New World trade as the captain of two slaving voyages that had earned their investors extraordinary profits. In defiance of Portugal's claim to a trade monopoly on the African continent, John Hawkins had sailed to the so-called Slave Coast (in the region of present-day Sierra Leone, Senegal, and Guinea), where he purchased or kidnapped black Africans to serve as slaves for the sugarcane plantations and mines of Spanish America.

This view of the city of Plymouth is a detail from what is known as the Henry VIII Defense Map, a document created on the order of that monarch in 1536 to aid him in determining what was needed to defend his realm from outside attack. Drake was born in the countryside near Plymouth around 1541; though his family moved away from the area when he was a youth, he moved back to the city as a young man and made it his home ever afterward.

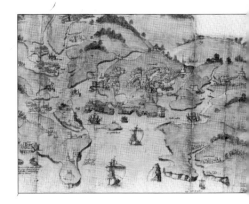

(The indignant Portuguese charged that Hawkins stole the slaves from their own slave ships.) Hawkins then sailed across the Atlantic to the New World, where he compelled the not always unwilling Spanish colonists—the settlers themselves often chafed at the Spanish Crown's restrictions on their commerce—to purchase his booty.

The 25-year-old Drake made his first voyage to the New World in 1566 as second-in-command under John Lovell, a captain of the Hawkins fleet. The voyage marked his initiation into the secrets of deep-sea navigation and ocean sailing, his first experience of the trade winds that blow almost continually toward the equator from the northeast and that would fill his sails on so many glorious occasions. Off the Slave Coast, he took part in his first raid on Portuguese ships and was tested in his first firefight at sea, and he felt for the first time the exultation of sailing away with the spoils of victory—highly valuable cargoes of slaves, ivory, wax, and sugar that he would help trade up and down the coasts of a forbidden territory.

But in the Spanish Main—the waters of the Caribbean and the coastal regions of South and Central America that adjoin them—Drake learned a little of some of the perils of pirating. At Rio de la Hacha, a small port on the Caribbean coast of what is today the nation of Colombia, Lovell's expedition was denied permission to trade by the town's officials. Hawkins's method had been to coerce the Spanish to trade by a show of force, but Lovell was not sufficiently equipped to do so, and he was forced to abandon many of his slaves and return to England with no profit to show for them.

Drake returned to the Caribbean in early 1568 as an officer under John Hawkins. Hawkins's fleet this time consisted of six vessels—among them two warships belonging to Queen Elizabeth, the 700-ton *Jesus of Lubeck* and the smaller *Minion*—that carried more than 400 men. The queen's interest in the voyage was the same as the syndicate of wealthy and well-born investors who backed it—profit. The royal treasury was overdrawn, and Elizabeth was reluctant to raise taxes. Many of the great English maritime expeditions of the Elizabethan Age were financed through a combination of private and royal investment, and Elizabeth counted on such ventures to help replenish the royal coffers. At the same time, she was also leery of antagonizing Spain and would, if necessary, be quick to deny complicity in the venture if Philip were to take offense. Accordingly, she pretended to believe Hawkins's disingenuous assurances that he would sail nowhere near Spain's New World colonies, warned him of her displeasure should he do so, and imparted as much to the Spanish ambassador.

The usual combination of piracy of Portuguese vessels and attacks on African villages enabled Hawkins and his men to fill the holds of their ships with some 500 slaves from Africa's west coast. Seven weeks' sailing brought them, in late March 1568, to the coast of Venezuela, where at Borburata the size and strength of their fleet convinced the reluctant Spanish officials to trade, and then westward to Rio de la Hacha. There, Drake, who had sailed ahead of the rest of the fleet in command of the *Judith*, bombarded the governor's home with shot and terrorized the harbor for several days until his companion vessels arrived—first evidence of the audacity that would characterize his maritime career. When Hawkins's demand for permission to trade was denied by the authorities, the English landed and sacked the town; after several days, the Spanish agreed to purchase several hundred slaves from the raiders and paid a huge ransom in gold as inducement for the English to leave. A similar sequence of events took place farther west at Santa Marta, although Cartagena was better defended and proved able to fend off the pirates.

Their holds filled with gold, silver, and pearls, the eight English ships—the corsairs had seized two Portuguese vessels off Africa—now prepared to return home. Hawkins set their course to the northwest, intending to take them around Cuba's west end and then east between that island and Florida, but in August the stormy season's first gales

The first English slave trader, John Hawkins was a kinsman— usually described as a cousin, although the exact relation is uncertain—of Drake's. His family was considerably more affluent and distinguished than Drake's; his father, William, was one of Plymouth's first citizens, a one-time mayor of the city and member of Parliament as well as a successful ship's captain and merchant who bequeathed to his two sons a small fleet of vessels.

drove them deep into the Gulf of Mexico. The *Jesus* was hit particularly hard; gaping holes were torn in its sides and its masts and rigging were damaged, and Hawkins was forced to head for the Spanish port of San Juan de Ulúa to make repairs.

San Juan de Ulúa was the settlement of Veracruz's outlet to the Gulf of Mexico. Like most of Spain's other ports in the New World, it was sparsely inhabited and poorly defended. Spain's military commitments in Europe left it short of manpower in the Americas, and what few soldiers it could spare for its overseas colonies were often employed inland to force the Indians into slavery in the mines and on the plantations. Until a short time previous, Spain had also had little reason to worry about defending its colonies, for few had dared challenge its might in the Americas.

San Juan de Ulúa's greatest importance was as the destination of one of the two yearly *flotas* (fleets) that sailed each spring from Spain to the New World. These flotas—

Spanish Tyranny in the West Indies is the title of this 16th-century Dutch engraving that depicts various atrocities committed by the Spanish against the native inhabitants of the New World. The undeniable cruelties perpetrated by the Spanish in the Americas inspired much of the anti-Catholic and anti-Spanish propaganda promulgated by Spain's Protestant enemies in England and the Netherlands.

Twenty-two years after Hawkins and Drake met disaster there, a Spanish military man drew this sketch of San Juan de Ulúa, a fortified low island in the Bay of Campeche that served as a harbor for the city of Veracruz. Though Drake and the English regarded the Spanish surprise attack there as unforgivable treachery—"You are not behaving like a gentleman," Hawkins shouted to one of the Spanish admirals as the ambush unfolded—the Spanish believed that they owed no honor to pirates. "I am following my vocation as a fighter," the Spanish admiral replied to Hawkins.

the other made for Nombre de Dios, on the Isthmus of Panama—consisted of cargo vessels escorted by warships and on the outward voyage carried a year's worth of food and clothing and other necessary supplies. On their return, they carried back to Spain the silver, gold, and precious stones that were to be found in such abundance in the Americas and that were the basis of Spain's power and wealth.

Hawkins's battered fleet arrived in San Juan de Ulúa just several days ahead of the flota. The English captain succeeded in convincing the officials of Veracruz that his intentions were peaceful and that he and his countrymen would leave as soon as they made the necessary repairs, but the arrival of the flota, which consisted of 2 warships and 11 armed merchant vessels and carried the new viceroy of Mexico, Martín Enríquez, complicated matters.

In later years, Drake regarded these circumstances as having offered a priceless opportunity, but Hawkins was more cautious. His ships occupied the protected harbor and could easily prevent the Spanish fleet from entering, leaving it to the mercy of the prevailing north winds, which would either drive the warships and galleons helplessly before it or, if the Spanish were less lucky, dash them on the rocks along the coast. ("Unless the ships be very carefully moored . . . there is no remedy for these north winds but death," Hawkins wrote in his account of the

The Jesus of Lubeck, Hawkins's *flagship on his 1568 voyage, was huge and well armed but also old (it had been purchased from German owners by Elizabeth's father, Henry VIII) and so leaky that by the time the English put in at San Juan de Ulúa its planks "did open and shut with every sea" and fish were found swimming in its hold.*

voyage.) Within the town's flimsy storehouses lay the year's shipment of bullion to Spain, that year's share of the fabulous treasure that had made Philip the most powerful monarch on the globe.

But the English already carried a rich cargo, and Hawkins realized that an attack on the flota would likely result in war between England and Spain, a consequence far exceeding the limits of what Elizabeth would countenance. He therefore only asked for guarantees that his own ships would not be attacked if he allowed the Spanish into the harbor and sent a message to Enríquez, "giving him to understand that before I would suffer them to enter the port, there would be some order of conditions pass between us, for our safe-being there, and maintenance of peace." An understanding was reached: the English could repair and restock their ships and depart unmolested, while the Spanish could proceed with their business without fearing any trouble or malice. The Spanish ships moored beside the English vessels in the harbor and hostages were exchanged, to be released when the English prepared to set sail.

The Spanish had no intention of abiding by the agreement. The English were in their territory, and Enríquez regarded their presence as an affront to the authority he had crossed the ocean to impose. Soldiers from the interior were smuggled onto the Spanish ships under cover of darkness, and on September 23, when all was ready, an attack was launched. Furious hand-to-hand fighting with pikes, swords, and muskets gave way to close-range cannonades as the English ships struggled out of boarding range. Only Hawkins's and Drake's seamanship enabled the English fleet to survive; well-placed shots from the *Jesus* and the *Minion* sank the Spanish flagship and exploded the powder magazine in the other warship, leaving it a flaming inferno from which scorched, screaming sailors leaped into the roiling waters of the harbor. Drake directed his ship, the *Judith*, to the rescue of the now-crippled *Jesus*, where Hawkins, silver cup of beer in hand, was urging, in the words of one who was on deck, "the gunners to stand by their ordnance lustily like men" and directing the evacuation of his other sailors onto the *Minion*. Drake's ship also began taking off men and treasure, until the appearance of a Spanish fire ship—an abandoned vessel, set ablaze and on a collision course with the enemy ships—caused "a marvellous fear." Having loaded its fill, the *Judith* had already pulled away; now the *Minion* began to do so. Hawkins and others leaped to safety aboard its decks; others fell short and drowned in the harbor or were captured by the Spanish; the remainder were left behind aboard the doomed *Jesus*. The *Judith* and the *Minion* fought their way out of the harbor; the remaining English vessels were captured or sunk.

In the confusion that followed the battle, the two surviving English ships were separated, probably because Drake, from fear of the rocky coast, took his vessel out to sea. Hawkins's vessel was so overloaded that half of those on board chose to be put ashore rather than risk the voyage home; most, no doubt, fell victim to the Spanish or the Native Americans. Dozens more died of sickness or their wounds on the trip back; only 80 of the more than 400 men who sailed with the fleet ever returned to their homeland. Humiliated, deprived of his treasure and glory, Hawkins accused Drake of willfully abandoning him and his men.

It was to be the only time in that mariner's career, henceforth characterized by a reckless audacity, that anyone would accuse Drake of cowardice. From him, there would be no forgiveness of Spain for the treachery at San Juan de Ulúa. From this time onward, virtually all of his exceedingly great energies would be devoted to exacting revenge on King Philip, the Catholic "Anti-Christ," as Drake called him. When, finally, Drake's piratical depredations succeeded in moving his nation and Spain from their diplomatically concealed enmity to outright war, it was simply an escalation of the personal battle he had taken upon himself to wage since that bloody day of betrayal and death in the small harbor of San Juan de Ulúa.

According to his biographer George Malcolm Thomson, "the covert struggle with Spain" to which Drake devoted himself after the debacle at San Juan de Ulúa "was a passage of arms in a holy war, the preliminary skirmishes of an inevitable battle." The evident advantages possessed by his enemy did not daunt Drake, who believed that he could use his superior seamanship to strike at the most vulnerable areas of Philip's empire.

The Treasure
House of
the World

The miseries and troublesome affairs of the sorrowful
voyage" (Hawkins's description in his published account)
put Elizabeth at odds with her mariners. Hawkins and
Drake were both quick to demand authorization for a
voyage of reprisal against the Spanish colonies, but the
queen was more cautious. Elizabeth wanted to force Philip
into allowing English shipping to trade at his New World
ports, but she did not want to go to war over the issue; she
wished to provoke, but not outrage, the Spanish monarch.
Her actions were always informed by a shrewd understanding of the necessities of state, whereas Drake's undeniable patriotism was fueled by a sense of personal injury
and intense religious zealotry that made him, for the
queen's purposes, just the slightest bit unreliable, for after
San Juan de Ulúa he recognized no limits in his personal
war with Spain.

Tormented by the Spanish treachery, his own disgrace
(Hawkins's account of the voyage had made it clear that
he felt Drake had cravenly abandoned him), and the
reports of the torture undergone by those of his countrymen
who had fallen into Spanish hands—whippings, enslave-
ment, hanging, and even crucifixion were the lot of those
prisoners who refused to embrace Catholicism—Drake became a pirate. French and Dutch mariners had for many
years preyed on Spanish shipping in the English Channel,

*The Huguenot pirate and explorer
Guillaume le Testu, Drake's partner
at Nombre de Dios, created this map
of the West Indies and the eastern
portion of North America in 1555,
one year before the publication of
his atlas,* Universal Cosmography.
*By the time he combined forces with
Drake, Le Testu had supervised the
founding of the first French colony
in Brazil and had been imprisoned
by the Spanish for several years as
a result of his privateering.*

but Drake, with the audacity that was his most outstanding characteristic, had a different approach in mind. He had been to the Caribbean and seen firsthand the complacency with which Spain attended to the defense of its ports there. He knew as well the importance of the New World's gold and silver to Philip's ability to maintain his empire, and he came to believe that Hawkins had missed a rare opportunity in his encounter with the flota. Others could worry about forcing the Spanish to trade; Drake would simply take what he wanted, dealing Philip a painful blow in the process. Philip Nichols, Protestant clergyman and the author of *Sir Francis Drake Revived*, a biographical account written in 1592 (most probably at Drake's urging and possibly with his involvement) and published by Drake's nephew and namesake some 30 years later, described what motivated Drake after San Juan de Ulúa: "There is a particular indignation engrafted in the bosom of all that are wronged, which ceaseth not seeking by all means possible to redress or remedy the wrong received. . . . [he set out for the Spanish Main] to gain such intelligence as might further him to get some amend for his loss . . . not only in the loss of goods of some value, but also of his kinsmen and friends."

In early 1570, Drake left Mary Newman, his bride of only a few months—prolonged separations would be the hallmark of their marriage—to make his first raid in the New World. His initial venture seems not to have been particularly profitable except in terms of information gathered. With the instinct of a born pirate, Drake singled out Nombre de Dios, a sleepy jungle outpost on the Caribbean coast of the Isthmus of Panama, as the focus of his attention. A storm-ridden collection of about 200 wooden houses arrayed around an open, poorly defended bay, Nombre de Dios was also arguably Spain's most important Caribbean port.

The treasure house of the world, Drake called it, for Nombre de Dios was the destination of the second flota

that sailed from Spain each year. There, after the supplies had been unloaded from the huge cargo ships, their holds were filled with all the gold and silver taken from Spain's South American mines in the previous year. From Potosí, the world's richest mine, and from other sites in what are now Peru and Bolivia, the bullion was carried up the west coast of South America in cumbersome, unguarded galleons to Panama, a small settlement on the Pacific coast of the isthmus. Trains of five or six hundred mules then transported the treasure along a muddy path through the rainy jungle to Venta Cruces, on the Chagres River, where some of it was transferred to small boats for shipment upstream to Nombre de Dios; the remainder was carried onward to that port by the plodding beasts of burden.

This 16th-century drawing portrays some of the silver mines at Potosí, in present-day Bolivia, which were the source of much of 16th-century Spain's wealth. The Spanish called the mountain range near Potosí the cerro rico— the rich hills.

Drake apparently did not raid any shipping or habitations on his 1570 voyage, but he was back in the Caribbean, captaining a ship called the *Swan*, early the next year. A Spanish frigate bound from Cartagena to Nombre de Dios was the first to feel his wrath. "We are surprised that you ran from us in that fashion," began the mocking note Drake left aboard the ransacked vessel, whose crew had fled in panic at the approach of the English. "Since you will not come courteously to talk with us . . . you will find your frigate spoiled by your own fault. And to any who courteously may come to talk to us, we will do no harm, under our flag. And who does not come, his be the blame. . . . Done by English, who are well disposed if there be no cause to the contrary; if there be cause, we will be devils rather than men." Throughout his marauding days, Drake would almost always behave graciously toward those who capitulated to him, less so to those who resisted; overall, very few Spaniards suffered physical harm as a result of his raids.

An even more audacious feat followed the plundering of the frigate. With several pinnaces—small, masted vessels, usually designed so that they could be broken down and stored in the hold of a ship, then reassembled when needed—Drake proceeded up the Chagres River as far as Venta Cruces, where he seized a large quantity of trade goods and sank several small Spanish ships. The success of the raid constituted proof to Drake of the vulnerability of Spain's treasure route across the isthmus. Back in the Caribbean, he picked off another frigate and a dozen or so barks as they approached the mouth of the Chagres, making off with many slaves and much valuable merchandise. In between raids, the pirates sheltered in a pleasant bay east of Nombre de Dios that Drake named Port Pheasant for the abundance of those colorful game birds that could be found scurrying through the tropical underbrush there. While Spanish colonial officials were firing off panicky missives to Philip, pleading for more protection—"It is plain we are going to suffer from this corsair and others, unless Your Majesty apply the remedy hoped for, by sending a couple of galleys to protect and defend this coast and the town, which is in the greatest danger"—and wondering where the diabolical Englishman would appear next, Drake was busy caching supplies at Port Pheasant in preparation for his next exploit and making ready to return to England. By the time he set sail late in 1571, Drake knew every inlet and shallow of the coast of the Spanish Main as well as every street, fortified landmark, and inland access route of Nombre de Dios.

In fulfillment of the worst fears of the Spanish, by July 1572 Drake had returned for a third time to the Spanish Main. He brought with him 73 men, distributed between two ships, the *Pasco* and the *Swan* (captained by his brother John), which made the crossing in a mere 25 days—testimony to Drake's rapid mastery of open-sea navigation, which, because of the absence of visible landmarks, called for a much different set of skills than he had learned in his Channel apprenticeship. The Port Pheasant hideout had been discovered in his absence, but he set his eager young crew (all but one were less than 30 years old) to work reclearing land for their settlement, building a fort, and assembling three pinnaces. Morale was exceptional, buoyed by the expectancy of adventure and riches; Drake encouraged the high spirits by setting aside ample time for recreation, usually in the form of archery contests and games of lawn bowling. Living by their wits on the raw jungle edge of a new world colonized by a powerful enemy, Drake's men contentedly made preparations to heist a year's worth of the treasure produced in the South American mines.

Most of Drake's strategies relied for their success on the almost unthinkable boldness, the borderline recklessness, of their designs, and his first attempt at Nombre de Dios was no exception. Three hundred and sixty tons of silver and a greater value of gold lay in the treasure house of the world as the dawn (and the English) approached in the early morning hours of July 29. Drake's perfectly executed surprise attack created havoc; his archers used flaming

By 1570, there were large cimarrón *populations in most of Spain's New World dominions. According to one of Drake's men, the cimarrones on the Isthmus of Panama welcomed the opportunity to help the English as a chance "to revenge the wrongs and injuries which the Spanish nation had done them." The Spanish greatly feared such an alliance because, wrote a Panama civic official, "being so thoroughly acquainted with the region and so expert in the bush, the Negroes will show them [the English] methods and means to accomplish any evil design they wish to carry out and execute."*

arrows to set fire to several buildings, his trumpeters "bl[e]w lustily" from various corners, and his drummers pounded away at several different locations. The intent was to confuse the Spanish, who greatly outnumbered Drake's small force, as to the size and direction of the attack.

In concept and operation the strategy was brilliant. The hastily assembled Spanish militia presented only token resistance and soon broke and fled, although Drake did suffer a rather serious leg wound from a musket ball. In a short time, the English found themselves in the governor's house, where a pile of bars of silver, 70 feet long, 10 feet wide, and 12 feet high, stood against one wall. After hefting a few for weight—40 pounds apiece, the pirates guessed—the English rushed on to the waterfront storehouse where the greater part of Nombre de Dios's wealth was kept. There, as Drake raged futilely at the thick, barred doors of the storehouse—"he had brought them to the mouth of the treasure of the world," he is reported telling his men in *Sir Francis Drake Revived*, "if they would want it, they might henceforth blame nobody but themselves"—they were stopped. Blood was pouring from Drake's leg, and his men, aware that the Spanish were regrouping, insisted on returning him to the safety of the ship. Left behind was all the treasure of Nombre de Dios—a fabulous price to pay for their captain's life, but one that his loyal followers apparently deemed worth it, for they believed, according to *Sir Francis Drake Revived*, that so long as they "had him to command them, they might recover wealth sufficient; but if once they lost him, they should hardly be able to recover home."

The English retreated to a group of small islands west of Nombre de Dios. Their leader made a quick recovery and was soon directing his band eastward to Cartagena, where he seized and burned an unladen ship and generally menaced the harbor, to no great effect other than the consternation of the city's inhabitants. After scuttling the *Swan* (the pinnaces had proved more useful), the pirates then proceeded south to the Gulf of Urabá, where they established a stronghold similar to the one at Port Pheasant. At the instigation of a black man named Diego, a former slave of the Spanish who had come over to the English during the raid on Nombre de Dios, Drake now determined to make contact with the *cimarrones*, as the Spanish called those blacks who had escaped from slavery for a life of freedom in the mountains and wilderness, where they established their own communities. From his haven in the Gulf of Urabá, Drake made several successful sorties against Spanish shipping, obtaining thereby the provisions necessary to feed his men. Meanwhile, with Diego as the intermediary, he succeeded in contacting the cimarrones, who expressed their eagerness to join in an action against the Spanish and provided the English with much valuable information about the movements of the treasure trains across the isthmus.

It was now September, the onset of the rainy season, when the movements of the treasure trains ceased. Drake had five months to lay his plans, and he decided to occupy some of his time in bedeviling Cartagena again. With several pinnaces, he succeeded in blockading the harbor for several months, to the steadily rising fury of the city fathers. He finally quit the port in early November, driven away only by the need to resupply. In the meantime, back in the Gulf of Urabá, his brother John, who possessed some of the same reckless spirit as his oldest sibling, had perished in an ill-advised attack on a Spanish frigate. Not long after Drake's return, another brother, Joseph, died during one of the periodic epidemics of tropical diseases—the culprit this time was probably yellow fever—that were the bane of Europeans in the New World. Drake himself performed an autopsy on Joseph, who had died in his arms, but he received no insight into the cause of the disease, which so ravaged the English that they named the body of land where they had built their stockade Slaughter Island.

These tragedies only strengthened Drake's resolution to avenge himself on the Spanish. Sometime in January 1573, a party of cimarrón scouts arrived at Drake's hideaway with the welcome news that the flota had put in at Nombre de Dios; in a short time the treasure trains would be crossing the isthmus. And with 30 cimarrones and 18 of the 23 English who had survived the epidemic, so, too, would be Drake.

As always, his plan hinged on surprise. The Spanish would naturally expect so insolent a corsair to attack from the sea, and their greatest concern was with the safety of the flota. But Drake had recognized that the treasure was most vulnerable when it was being carried across the isthmus, a point confirmed for him by the cimarrones, and he intended to make his move on it by land.

Guided by the cimarrones, his sea dogs crossed the central cordilleras (chains of mountains) that run east-west across the isthmus and made their way through the steamy jungles of the interior. On the fourth day of their march, at the summit of a ridge, the cimarrones guided Drake to an exceptionally tall tree fitted with a platform in its upper branches. After climbing to this platform, Drake was able to see both the Caribbean Sea to the north and to the south the vast, unknown expanse of the Pacific Ocean. Drake was probably the first Englishman to gaze upon the Pacific; he is said to have dropped to his knees at the sight, uttered a prayer in which he "besought almighty God of his goodness to give him life and leave to sail once in an English ship in that sea," and vowed to "sail thither and make a perfect discovery" of the Pacific. "From that time forward, his mind was pricked on continually night and day to perform this vow," wrote Nichols in *Sir Francis Drake Revived.* John Oxenham, who had succeeded John Drake as second-in-command, was equally impressed. The taciturn Oxenham, who had clambered up the tree behind Drake, now swore to accompany him to the Pacific; he "protested that unless our captain did beat him from his company he would follow him by God's grace."

Soon after, the raiders descended the mountain slopes to the open pampas (plains) that lay between the settlements

of Venta Cruces and Panama. One of the cimarrones snuck into Panama and learned that the fleet from Peru had already arrived; two mule trains, one loaded with silver and gold and the other with provisions, were scheduled to set out for Venta Cruces in the cool of that very evening.

Drake laid his ambush at the midpoint between the two cities. The tinkling of the mules' bells was to signal a general attack, but a drunken pirate who sprang prematurely from the cover of the brush was sighted by a rider from Venta Cruces; the horseman galloped ahead to warn the mule trains' leaders, who sent ahead only the caravan of provisions. Drake and his men had no choice but to retire

French pirates plunder a Spanish settlement in the New World in this 1598 Dutch engraving. French corsairs began attacking Spain's American colonies as early as the 1520s, and Huguenot merchants often commissioned English seamen to raid Spanish shipping in the English Channel.

Llamas transport silver from the Potosí mines in this 1602 engraving by Theodor de Bry, a Flemish engraver and goldsmith who illustrated the accounts of many New World travelers. The Spanish, who called them Peruvian sheep, used llamas as beasts of burden only in the Andean regions of South America; the riches of the treasure train waylaid by Drake and Le Testu on the isthmus were carried by an Old World pack animal—the mule.

as quickly as possible to the safety of the Caribbean, although they consoled themselves in retreat by sacking Venta Cruces.

Back aboard his pinnaces, Drake spent about a month raiding Spanish shipping, hoping to convince his enemies that he had returned his attention to the sea. In the course of his depredations, he met up with Guillaume Le Testu, a Huguenot (French Protestant) privateer of considerable repute. In addition to his raids on Spanish settlements in the West Indies, Le Testu had made several exploratory voyages to Brazil—his *Universal Cosmography*, published in 1556, featured some of the earliest French maps of the Americas—and was one of the first to export the New World product of tobacco to Europe. The two captains

knew and admired each other by reputation; their parley in the Caribbean was preceded by an exchange of elegant gifts. The French pirate gave his English counterpart a case of pistols and a gilt scimitar; Drake responded with a gold chain. From Le Testu, Drake learned of the St. Bartholomew's Day Massacre: at the instigation of the French royal family, 50,000 Huguenots had been slain by Catholics in France the previous August. The grim news reconfirmed Drake in his sense of mission against all things Catholic (and by extension, Spanish). Le Testu shared Drake's animus; he was in the Caribbean to raid Spanish shipping and perform reconnaissance for a proposed French invasion of the West Indies.

The two likeminded mariners agreed to combine their forces for another assault on the treasure trains. Early in April, a force of 20 French, 20 cimarrones, and 15 English landed at the Francisca River, a day's march east through the jungle to Nombre de Dios. On the Campos River, about a mile from the treasure house of the world, Drake and Le Testu laid their ambush. This time, the attack caught the Spanish completely by surprise, and the 45-man escort of soldiers fled down the trail, abandoning the mule train, which was carrying 25 tons of silver and 100,000 pesos of gold. (The gold alone was the equivalent of $5 million today.)

Recognizing that the routed escort would soon alert Nombre de Dios and return with help, the victorious raiders buried most of the silver and made off with as much gold as they could carry. On arriving at the designated rendezvous at the Francisca moorage, however, they were shocked to find Spanish ships rather than their own riding at anchor offshore.

Concealing his fear that the Spanish had captured his trusty pinnaces, Drake, with his customary bravado, insisted that the pinnaces had simply been stalled by contrary winds and ordered his frantic men to assemble a raft from whatever driftwood and logs they could lay their hands on.

The raft, he explained, would be sailed to sea in search of the missing ships. As described in *Sir Francis Drake Revived*, "the raft was fitted and fast bound; a sail of bisquit sack prepared; an oar was shaped out of a young tree to serve instead of a rudder. . . . In this manner putting off to sea, he sailed some three leagues [about 10 miles], sitting up to the waist continually in water, and at every surge of the wave to the armpits." In a secure cove to the east, Drake and the three volunteers who had accompanied him—an Englishman and two Frenchmen—found his pinnaces. The astonished men aboard assumed that Drake's drenched and ragged clothes and the size of his party denoted disaster—until, with a wicked grin, the captain pulled a ring of gold from his clothing. With his pinnaces, he returned to the Francisca to pick up his men. Le Testu had died from a wound sustained in the raid and the buried silver was gone, but an astonishing amount of gold—equal to about one-fifth of the English crown's annual income and roughly equal to $3 million in today's currency—was theirs to take home.

The "humble English captain," as Drake called himself, had won the first battle in his one-man war against Philip's Catholic empire. On his way home, he could not resist a brief detour; with the cross of St. George flying from each topsail and silk banners fluttering from his ship's bow and each cross spar, Drake paraded his victory by sailing tauntingly back and forth at the mouth of Cartegena's "impenetrable" harbor. Behind him, as he set sail across the Atlantic, the denizens of Spain's colonial outposts trembled. "This realm is at the moment so terrified," wrote the Municipal Council of Panama to Philip, "and the spirits of all so disturbed, that we know not in what words to emphasize to your Majesty the solicitude we make in this dispatch, for we certainly believe that if remedial action be delayed, disaster is imminent. . . . These English have so shamelessly opened the door and a way by which, with impunity, whenever they desire, they will attack the pack-

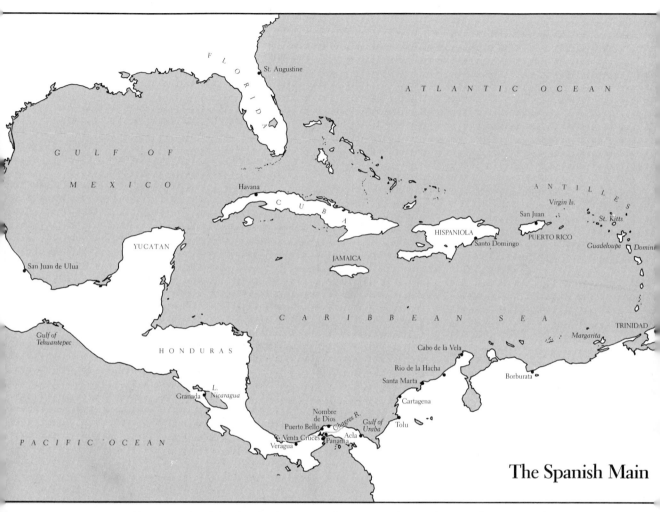

The Spanish Main

The Spanish Main was the scene of some of Drake's most daring and lucrative exploits.

trains travelling overland by this highway." Other Spanish put it more simply. Francis Drake is the devil, they said—words that would be repeated time and again in the years to come.

The Voyage of the Century

The 1570s were a time of great interest in maritime enterprise in England. Spain and Portugal's example had demonstrated the benefits to be gained from overseas exploration, and Drake's exploits indicated to Elizabeth and her advisors that it might be possible for England to develop a more ambitious naval strategy. Economic interests dictated an expansion of England's maritime commerce; unemployment was high at home, the country was overpopulated, many segments of the population were hungry, and England's traditional trade with northern Europe had fallen off. Investors and merchants were constantly seeking new overseas markets and opportunities outside the scope of the Spanish and Portuguese monopolies. Companies were formed to promote the exploration and development of new trade routes to Russia, via the Norwegian and Barents seas, and to China via the Northwest Passage, a purported waterway through the upper reaches of North America, well north of Spain's claims in the New World.

Attention was focused on the New World's southern climes as well. John Dee, a Welsh scientist and wizard with considerable influence at Elizabeth's court (he was the queen's friend and personal astrologer), championed the purported existence of an enormously vast, undiscovered continent rich with gold in the uncharted seas below South America. The owner of the largest library in England, Dee combined considerable scientific acumen and knowledge with a reliance on the occult. He called this undiscovered

A 1560 engraving of a Spanish merchant ship. Such ships were designed for cargo-carrying capacity, not maneuverability, which made them easy prey for the smaller, nimbler vessels captained by Drake and his like.

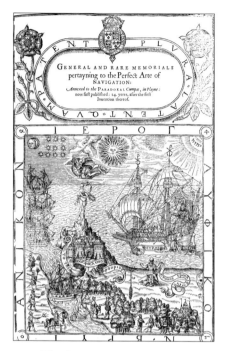

The frontispiece to a 16th-century edition of John Dee's Brityshe Complement of the Perfect Art of Navigation, *which the Welshman dedicated to Christopher Hatton. If it was Dee who foresaw that maritime endeavors would be the means by which his country could lay claim to an "incomparable Brityshe empire," it was Drake who did more than any individual of the day to fulfill that vision.*

land mass Terra Australis Incognita—Latin for the "unknown southern land"—and predicted that it would outdo in riches all the new lands discovered by Europeans in the last century or so, for it was his proposition that the heat of the sun generated precious metals, gems, and spices in the southern regions.

Dee expounded this and other theories in his 1577 treatise, *The Brityshe Complement of the Perfect Art of Navigation*, wherein he predicted a newfound greatness for tiny and traditionally impoverished England. The magus foresaw an "Incomparable Brityshe Empire" that would, by means of "tolerance and justice," peacefully resolve the painful divisions wrought in Europe by the struggle between Catholicism and Protestantism—a prediction that accorded with Elizabeth's vision of her kingdom's destiny.

The chief obstacle to Elizabeth's dreams of empire remained Philip. The personal affection that the two monarchs felt for one another was incompatible with their personal religious commitments and England's and Spain's strategic and economic interests. In 1559, Philip had sworn before 200,000 of his subjects "to defend the holy Catholic faith with all the strength of his empire"; though he had lived in England for six years, he was unable to regard Protestantism as anything other than a monstrous heresy. Elizabeth was no less committed to her faith and the well-being of its practitioners, particularly in the Netherlands, where the Protestant opposition to Spanish rule did her the service of forcing Philip to commit money and manpower there that he could ill afford. The destruction of the Dutch city of Antwerp by Spanish forces in 1576 infuriated her, though she was uncertain as to what steps should be taken in response.

Always prudent, though appreciative of boldness; shrewdly cognizant of Spain's strength, though eager to exploit its weaknesses, Elizabeth presided over a similarly divided council of advisers. Chief among this extraordinary array of talented men was William Cecil, the Lord Burghley, a hardworking and sober intellectual who had distinguished himself in Elizabeth's service even before her ascent to the throne; the queen's faith in his judgment rarely wavered. Though an investor in Hawkins's ill-fated voyage and several other trading and privateering ventures, Burghley counseled caution in regard to Spain, for as the nation's treasurer he feared that war would drive England into bankruptcy.

The members of the so-called war party among Elizabeth's advisers disparaged such discretion in favor of a more provocative policy. Foremost among these was Christopher Hatton, captain of the guard and one of the queen's favorites; Francis Walsingham, head of Elizabeth's secret police; and Robert Dudley, the Earl of Leicester. It was to these gentlemen that Drake, armed with letters of introduction from Robert Devereux, the Earl of Essex, in whose service he had spent some of the previous two years fighting rebels in Ireland, proposed a voyage through the Strait of Magellan, near the southern tip of South America, and then northward in the Pacific along the continent's west coast.

Drake's plan coincided with similar schemes then under consideration by Elizabeth's advisers. These ventures variously proposed the founding of colonies near the Strait of Magellan (the southern shore of which was believed to constitute the northern reaches of Terra Australis Incognita) and the establishment of trade with the natives of the southern regions of present-day Chile, which Spain had not yet occupied. Though, of necessity, Drake spoke of his venture only in the most guarded of terms, Walsingham, Leicester, and other possible backers would have immediately discerned its potential profitability and usefulness as an irritant to Philip. Drake was, after all, the impudent soul who had plundered the treasure house of the world.

Impressed by Drake's discretion in refusing to present him with a written list of places where Philip's empire was vulnerable—the queen was mortal, the mariner explained

Sir Christopher Hatton was the captain of the queen's bodyguard and a particular favorite of Elizabeth's, whose attention he had captured by his accomplished dancing at a court masque. His family crest, the golden hind (depicted in foreground), became the name of Drake's ship. Along with Francis Walsingham, the earls of Leicester and Lincoln, John Hawkins, and George and William Winter (members of a famous seagoing family), Hatton was one of the most important supporters of Drake's South American voyage, in which he, like the others, invested heavily.

In this romanticized conception, Drake points out to Elizabeth and her advisers the Pacific regions of South America where he believed Philip's empire to be most vulnerable. In actuality, it is uncertain how forthcoming Drake was regarding his actual intentions, though there can be little doubt that those who invested in the voyage (Elizabeth among them, claimed Drake) understood that their money was to be recouped and multiplied through attacks on Spanish shipping.

while pointing on a map to the west coast of Philip's South American dominions, and should she be succeeded by an individual favorably disposed to Philip, "then will my own hand be a witness against myself"—Walsingham arranged for him to meet Elizabeth. "I would gladly be revenged on the King of Spain for divers injuries that I have received," Drake recorded her as saying to him, "and you are the only man that might do this exploit." Encouraged, Drake (according to his own account) then revealed to her his plan for attacking Spanish shipping in the Pacific after passing through the Strait of Magellan. Despite the piratical nature of the proposal, the queen agreed to it, though nothing to that effect was placed in writing, for fear of implicating her with Philip. "If need be, the gentleman careth not if I should disavow him," Elizabeth wrote about a similar sub-

terfuge required of a later endeavor of hers and Drake's; the sentiment applies equally well to their first arrangement. Though the queen invested a substantial sum of money with the syndicate backing Drake, she would not allow any royal ships to be part of his fleet.

Deception and secrecy marked the preparation for the voyage, for word about the true nature of the mission had to be kept not only from Philip's many spies in England but from Burghley and the more conciliatory of Elizabeth's own advisers. "I hate all pirates mortally," Burghley had been quoted as saying. "Of all men my Lord Treasurer should not know it," Elizabeth said to Drake in discussing the true nature of his mission. Not even the sailors recruited by Drake and his captains to man their ships were to know their actual destination; they were led to believe that they were signing on for a trading voyage to the Levant, while the gentlemen who sailed with him apparently believed that the expedition was essentially sailing in search of Terra Australis Incognita.

Preparations for the voyage began in the summer of 1576 with the construction of what was to be Drake's flagship, the *Pelican*. Drake and his officers personally supervised every aspect of making ready. For his principal ships, Drake insisted on lead sheathing sandwiched between double oak hulls—extra protection should rock, reef, cannonball, or shipworm pierce the outer planking. Five ships in all fitted out for the voyage's original fleet: the *Pelican*, at 70 feet in length and 100 tons burden the largest of the vessels, and with 18 guns the best armed; the *Elizabeth*, 80 tons and 16 guns; the much smaller *Marigold*, 30 tons and 16 guns; the *Swan*, 50 tons and 5 guns; and the *Christopher*, 15 tons and 1 gun. A crew of 164 manned them—120 seamen, 12 officers, 15 gentlemen-adventurers, 10 soldiers, and several ship's boys. In their number were an apothecary, a shoemaker, a tailor, a preacher, and musicians to play trumpets, oboes, and viols during the long days of sailing and while the captain dined.

This 16th-century chart of the Strait of Magellan illustrates the prevailing geographical tenet—to be dispelled by Drake's voyage— that the strait constituted a narrow water passage between the two nearly contiguous continents of South America and Terra Australis Incognita. The search for the unknown southern continent was one of the ostensible purposes of Drake's voyage.

Drake, the officers, and the gentlemen would enjoy a certain degree of comfort and finery aboard their vessels. Carved oak tables and chairs, silk cushions and Turkish carpeting, silver platters and flatware, paintings, and an elaborate canopied bed for the captain's cabin were carried on board at Plymouth, along with the more mundane necessities of a long ocean voyage—barrels of biscuit, meal, beer, wine, beef, pork, fish, butter, cheese, rice, oatmeal, peas, vinegar, honey, salt, and gunpowder; wood, coal, candles, wax, lanterns, culinary utensils, compasses and other navigational instruments, fishing nets, hooks, and lines. One unique item was Drake's drum, a painted instrument that always traveled with the music-loving corsair like a mascot and was stowed in his cabin with terrestrial and celestial globes, a copy of Antonio Pigafetta's journal of Ferdinand Magellan's voyage of circumnavigation, sea charts (many of Spanish and Portuguese origin), books of navigation, and gifts from the queen for his journey: perfumes, sweets, and a sea cap with the blessing "The lord guide and preserve thee until the end" embroidered upon it in silk.

The *Pelican* led the way as Drake's ships departed Plymouth on a wintry December 13, 1577. The small fleet bore south at first, as would an expedition bound for the Middle East, but then sailed a course toward the coast off Morocco instead of entering the mouth of the Mediterranean. There, off Cape Blanco, the fleet commandeered a 40-ton Portuguese vessel, in favor of which the original *Christopher* was abandoned. (The prize was renamed the *Christopher*.) The English then sailed southwest toward the Cape Verde Islands, 500 miles due west from the African coast, the last place where fresh water or food could be taken on before the ocean crossing. En route, Drake surprised and captured a large Portuguese trading ship bound for Brazil with a cargo of fine fabrics and wines. Command of the new vessel, called the *Mary* by the English, was given to Thomas Doughty, who had served with Drake in Ireland and had emerged as the leader of the increasingly disgruntled contingent of gentlemen-adventurers. Drake put ashore all the Portuguese crew of the *Mary* except its veteran pilot, Nuño da Silva, who unwillingly spent the next 15 months as a useful and observant guest aboard the *Pelican*.

Da Silva's later recollections of Drake portray the Englishman as friendly and courteous in exchanges other than the giving of orders, of which Drake demanded precise and immediate obedience. His crew respected rather than feared him, and unless crossed he was usually generous and outgoing toward them. Unlike the gentlemen aboard, Drake did not hesitate to perform any task necessary (the gentlemen believed themselves exempt from manual labor), and he did not believe that pitching in endangered his authority. Da Silva judged his kidnapper to be an already exemplary seaman and praised his hunger to expand his knowledge of navigation.

The Portuguese pilot's experience soon proved a valuable asset. Having never before sailed this far south, Drake and his men were unprepared for the Doldrums, a perplexing stretch of calm waters, dead air, squalls, and light, baffling breezes just north of the equator where ships were frequently becalmed. Though da Silva provided reassurances that such conditions were not unusual, the absence of winds and the stifling equatorial heat only added to the discontent already evident among some members of Drake's crew.

Dissension was not unusual on long voyages; the close quarters aboard ship and the stress arising from journeying in unknown waters made it all but inevitable at some point, which is why the character of the commander was of such critical importance. Drake had several potential sources of discontent to contend with: his small ships were exceptionally crowded, and virtually all of those aboard had been deceived about the nature, length, and destination of the voyage. Murmuring had begun virtually as soon as Drake had steered his fleet away from the Mediterranean, but he succeeded in winning most of the crew over to him. Like the seamen and soldiers, Drake was a commoner; he understood their fears and concerns, and his style of command, his usual good cheer, and his flair and daring earned their loyalty. He fared less well with his gentlemen—and with Thomas Doughty in particular.

The cause of the antagonism between Drake and Doughty has been much speculated upon. Initially, the two men were friends, and the well-connected Doughty may have aided Drake in planning his voyage by introducing him to Christopher Hatton. But like some of the other gentlemen aboard, Doughty had made a sizable investment in the venture, and he apparently believed that his financial backing entitled him to a greater say in the command of the fleet than Drake was willing to grant him. Indeed, several of the gentlemen aboard found Drake insufficiently deferential; the famous pirate was accustomed to keeping his own counsel, and though he was not totally adverse to hearing other opinions, he was just as likely to ignore them. Nor was he likely to consult with his officers before making decisions. Command by consensus was not Drake's style; some of those aboard no doubt found him maddeningly impetuous, if not downright reckless. Derek Wilson, one of Drake's many biographers, believes that trouble began because "those next in seniority to Drake were fired with enthusiasm for a voyage of exploration and discovery. They did not share his hatred of Spain, nor were they party to his piratical intentions. As their journey unfolded and their leader was gradually revealed as little more than a corsair, unbreachable rifts appeared in the command of the enterprise." Whether this was Doughty's complaint is unknown (as an investor, Doughty most likely knew of the voyage's secret objectives), but the great naval historian Sir Julian Corbett believed that Doughty was acting in Burghley's employ with orders to sabotage Drake's enterprise. However, according to the gossips in Plymouth following the voyage, the falling-out between the two men actually owed more to love than to court intrigue: Doughty and Mary Drake were having an affair, it was said, and in the Atlantic one night Doughty intemperately revealed his secret to the cuckold, whereupon each man resolved to destroy his rival.

Whatever its origins, the trouble began early in the voyage. After the taking of the *Mary*, Doughty was accused of pilfering some of the loot, in disregard of orders; he in turn accused Drake's brother Thomas of doing the same. Drake took no action; nonetheless, Doughty began muttering darkly about his friends and influence at court, his alleged ability as a sorcerer, and the possibility of making off with one of the ships to conduct his own raids. Further provocations followed; when Drake sent his trumpeter to Doughty's ship with a message, Doughty and his friends humiliated the man by "cobbeying" him—stripping him of his pants

Drake's drum accompanied him around the world in the Golden Hind. *His coat of arms was painted on its side after his return to England and his knighting by Elizabeth in 1581. The drum is 21 inches high and has a walnut shell; legend holds that in moments of great crisis for England, it can be heard beating to summon the spirit of its former owner to the rescue of the realm. Drake was the subject of many legends, both during his life and afterward. The Spanish believed, for example, that he possessed a magic mirror that showed him the exact location of every one of their ships at sea.*

Near a bay at almost 48 degrees south latitude, some of the native inhabitants of South America stole Drake's hat, a stylish scarlet model with a gold band. According to the Englishmen, these Indians were long-haired (unlike their depiction in this 16th-century engraving), painted themselves red, white, and black, went mostly unclad, loved music, and were quite friendly. Despite the theft, Drake "would suffer no man to hurt any of them," according to one of his shipmates.

and lashing him on the buttocks. Drake regarded the insult as aimed at him and relieved Doughty of his command, but aboard the *Swan*, where Drake ordered him transferred, Doughty continued to foment unrest by encouraging the gentlemen in their refusal to perform any work, engaging in a fistfight with the ship's master, boasting that he was responsible for Drake's exalted position, and telling the fleet's preacher that he would soon have all the men cutting each other's throats. The last comment moved Drake, once his ships, in May 1578, had reached an anchorage on the east coast of South America near 48 degrees south latitude, to have Doughty bound to the mainmast. Still, Doughty, once he was released for the resumption of the voyage southward, would not desist with his mutinous clamorings,

and the conflict culminated at a grim harbor named Port San Julián, 200 miles north of the entrance to the Strait. A grisly harbinger of the quarrel's resolution stood ashore there, among the rocks and scrub—a gibbet, dating from 58 years earlier, where Magellan had hanged the drawn and quartered bodies of two of his officers who had conspired against him.

In the biting cold of the South American winter, Drake convened a jury of 40 of Doughty's peers in a rough clearing on an uninhabited island in the bay of Port San Julián to hear charges against him. "You have here sought by diverse means, inasmuch as you may, to discredit me to the great hindrance and overthrow of this voyage, besides other great matters wherewith I have to charge you withal, the which if you can clear yourself of, you and I shall be very good friends, where to the contrary you have deserved death," Drake said to Doughty in opening the proceedings. The other "great matters" included charges of witchcraft; Doughty's knowledge of books and science caused many of the simple, illiterate sailors to regard him as having magical powers, and his brother, John, had boasted of their family's ability to "conjure as well as any men and that they could raise the devil and make him to meet any man in the likeness of a bear, a lion, or a man in [armor]." Many of the sailors believed that the mysterious becalming of their ships in the Doldrums had been the result of an evil spell.

Though Doughty was a lawyer, Drake overrode his objections to the lawfulness of the proceedings: "I have not to do with you crafty lawyers, neither care I for the law, but I know what I will do," he said. Several seamen testified about Doughty's incitements to mutiny, but the most damning evidence against him was his own admission that he had provided Burghley with knowledge of the expedition, which in Drake's opinion, in light of the instructions he had received from Elizabeth, constituted treason. The jury returned a unanimous verdict of guilty; Drake asked for and received the death penalty for the mutineer.

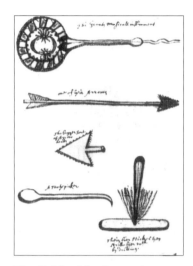

The Golden Hind's *preacher, Francis Fletcher, drew this picture of the weapons and tools carried by the Native Americans the Englishmen encountered near Port San Julián. Fletcher's narrative of the voyage formed the basis for much of* The World Encompassed.

According to Drake's own account of his preliminary discussions with Elizabeth regarding the circumnavigation voyage, the queen told him that above everything, Lord Burghley (pictured), the treasurer of the realm, was not to be provided with details about the expedition. Doughty's confession that he had given Burghley information about the voyage therefore sealed his fate. Though Burghley was among Elizabeth's most trusted public servants, he consistently counseled peaceful accommodation with Spain.

Doughty, who was allowed to choose his method of execution, asked to be beheaded—the gentleman's death.

The condemned took his last meal and Holy Communion with his judge two days later, on July 2. The two former friends dined in private and engaged in quiet discussion, "each cheering the other and taking their leave by drinking to each other." At the block, Doughty prayed aloud for his family and friends and for the success of the voyage, swore his innocence, asked his comrades to forgive him, and begged Drake not to carry out reprisals against any of his friends. Then he kneeled, and the ax fell. "Lo, this is the end of traitors," Drake pronounced as he displayed the bloody head to the solemn onlookers.

The execution did not immediately end the disquiet among Drake's men. Doughty had not been without friends, many of the gentlemen had not been enamored of Drake to begin with, and recent events had not inspired much confidence in the ultimate success of the voyage. No Englishman had ever before sailed these waters or visited these lands; very few mariners of any nationality, including the vaunted Spanish, had successfully navigated the Strait of Magellan. The fleet was to ride out the rest of the winter at desolate Port San Julián, affording the men much time for speculation, worry, and the cultivation of resentments.

On August 11, Drake addressed the situation. The men were assembled for a religious service, but when the preacher, Francis Fletcher, began his sermon, Drake interrupted. "Nay, soft Master Fletcher, I must preach this day," he said. Old quarrels must be laid to rest, said Drake, since "we are very far from our country and friends," soon to be in the waters of the enemy, and unable to obtain other men even should "we give for him ten thousand pounds." All must work together, he said, for

> I must have the gentleman to haul and draw with the mariner, and the mariner with the gentleman. Let us show ourselves all to be of a company, and let us not give occasion to the enemy to rejoice at our decay and

overthrow. . . . And as gentlemen are very necessary
for government's sake in the voyage, so have I shipped
them for that, and to some further intent, and yet
though I know sailors to be the most envious people of
the world, and so unruly without government, yet may
not I be without them.

Those who were unhappy were offered the use of the
Marigold and the opportunity to return home, "but let them
take heed that they go homeward, for if I find them in my
way I will surely sink them." "More there are who deserved
such a fate," he said in reference to the execution of
Doughty, "but as I am a gentleman, there shall no more die.
. . . And now, my masters, let us consider what we have
done . . . if this voyage should not have good success, we
should not only be a scorning or a reproachful scoffing stoke
unto our enemies, but also a great blot to our whole country
for ever, and what triumph would it be to Spain and
Portugal, and again the like would never be attempted."

The World Encompassed

None of Drake's men opted to return home, and within a week of his speech the fleet, now numbering three vessels (the *Swan* and the *Mary* had been burned to simplify logistics) had set sail for the Strait. The flagship had been rechristened the *Golden Hind*; Christopher Hatton, a former employer and patron of Doughty, displayed a gold-colored deer, or hind, on his coat of arms, and Drake hoped he might be flattered and appeased by the gesture.

In calm weather on the morning of August 24, the three ships made the outlying islands of the Strait of Magellan itself. For the first time Drake exercised the time-honored privilege of the explorer by giving names to two of these gateway islands: one became St. Bartholomew's, in observance of the saint whose feast day it was on the church calendar, and the other St. George's, "in honor of England, according to the ancient custom." The islands also offered the crew the opportunity to encounter penguins, described in *The World Encompassed*—an account of Drake's voyage compiled from various expedition narratives, primarily Fletcher's, and published by Drake's nephew in 1628—as "strange birds which could not fly at all." Their flightlessness made them easy pickings for the English sailors, who killed 3,000 of them in a single day, for according to *The World Encompassed* "they are a very good and wholesome victual." Thus stocked with fresh meat, the fleet entered the Strait.

The ceremonial barge of the sultan of Ternate is rowed out to greet Francis Drake and the Golden Hind. *The English stopped at Ternate after crossing the Pacific from the west coast of North America.*

Sailors hunt penguins near the Strait of Magellan; a 16th-century engraving. "They walk so upright that afar off a man would mistake them to be little children," was how penguins were described in The World Encompassed. *"In body they are less than a goose and bigger than a mallard, short and thick set together, having no feathers. . . . [I]n the space of one day we killed no less than 3,000."*

Navigating the Strait of Magellan was a formidable task, for the more than 300-mile-long channel is a veritable labyrinth of islands and passages, shoals, and deep water where Drake's ships were unable to anchor. Neither Drake nor anyone else aboard his ships, including the Portuguese pilot, had sailed these waters, and it is unlikely that whatever charts he possessed were of much use. On both coasts, recorded Fletcher, mountains "ar[o]se with such tops and spires into the air . . . as they may well be accounted amongst the wonders of the world." A variety of grasses and herbs grew on the craggy shores, which were accessible by "many small bays and coves . . . in which one could safely anchor." Drake made juice from several of these plants and mixed it with wine as a remedy for scurvy, which "nearly all" his men were suffering from; two died nonetheless. (The bane of seamen, scurvy results from vitamin C deficiency, which on long ocean voyages was caused by a lack of fresh food in the diet.) Despite often violently shifting winds, Drake took his fleet through the treacherous passage in just 16 days. Magellan, the strait's discoverer, had required 37, and two later 16th-century English mariners both took almost seven weeks.

On September 6, 1578, Drake's treetop wish "to sail once in an English ship on that sea" was fulfilled when his ships entered the Pacific. Fletcher observed that the Pacific might at that time have better been called the Furious Ocean, for a tremendous storm out of the north, "an intolerable tempest," carrying snow, rain, and fog on its raging winds, forbade Drake and his vessels from proceeding northward—as he had intended to do—very far along the coast of Chile. Driven by the storm, the ships instead retreated helplessly back to the south. Somewhere along that desolate coast, the *Marigold* sank, taking with it all its 29 hands. Aboard the *Golden Hind*, Fletcher, who had the watch, claimed to be able to hear, above the wind's shrieking, the "fearful cries" of the *Marigold*'s crew as their ship was "swallowed up with horrible & unmercifull waves"; the preacher attributed the disaster to divine retribution for Doughty's execution. Several days later, the *Elizabeth* became separated from the *Golden Hind* in "fog and outrageous winter." John Winter, the *Elizabeth*'s captain, skillfully guided his ship to safety inside the strait and then, either on his own inspiration or at the instigation of his crew, made sail for England, which he reached in June of the following year.

Drake's single, small, battered craft, now carrying 76 men, the only English ship in the vast Pacific, was all that remained of his once-proud fleet. The winds drove the *Golden Hind* southward until the last week of October, when it was able to anchor off a group of islands well south of the strait. Though the exact location and identity of these islands remains unknown, Drake was in the unexplored vicinity of Cape Horn, the southernmost point of South America. He himself believed he had reached the "utmost land of *terra incognita* [unknown land], to the southward of America" and named the archipelago the Elizabeth Isles, after his queen. On the southernmost of them, Drake erected a stone monument with the queen's name and the date on it, then stretched himself out on

Fletcher's drawing of an albatross, flying fish, a bonita, and a dolphin. Drake himself was an enthusiastic sketcher and painter of all that he encountered in the course of his voyage; unfortunately, none of his artwork has survived.

This late-16th-century world map by the Dutch engraver and cartographer Jodocus Hondius reflects some of the new geographical knowledge acquired as a result of Drake's circumnavigation of the world. Though Terra Australis Incognita is shown, the mapmaker has depicted open water between it and the southern end of South America. The west coast of South America just above the Strait of Magellan is shown trending less extremely northwest than had been previously believed, and the Strait of Anian is not portrayed (though a Northwest Passage above North America is depicted).

his stomach at the island's southernmost point so that he could claim that he had been farther south than any European before him. His fortuitous, undesired exploration of the southernmost climes of the western hemisphere enabled him to dispel the notion that Terra Australis existed south of the Strait of Magellan. The strait was not a passage between two continents at all; the land south of it was in fact several different islands, and it was possible to pass from the Atlantic to the Pacific through or to the south of them, the two oceans being there but "one and the self same sea," as Fletcher put it. In future years, this route from the Atlantic to the Pacific and vice versa—around South America via Cape Horn or nearby waters—would be known as the Drake Passage.

The storm that had blown the *Golden Hind* south for fiftysome days finally ceased, and while hugging the coast on the way back north, Drake made another important

geographic discovery. Most of the nautical charts and maps of the day depicted Chile's coast trending northwest, but Drake found that it ran almost due north and south for almost a thousand miles above the Strait. By November 25, he had reached Mocha Island, about 50 miles off the coast of central Chile at approximately 38 degrees south latitude, where he sent a landing party ashore in search of fresh water and food.

The only Europeans the islanders, who were probably members of the Araucanian tribe, had ever seen were Spaniards, and they assumed that the English had also come with the intent of enslaving them. The landing party was attacked as it took on fresh water, and a gunner and Diego, the cimarrón from the Isthmus of Panama who had returned with Drake to England as his personal attendant, were killed; 13 other Englishmen, including Drake, were wounded. Even so, Drake refused to allow the *Golden Hind*'s cannons to be trained on the Araucanians. The natives' action was understandable, he argued, for they had no doubt suffered unspeakable cruelties at the hands of the Spanish, for whom they had mistaken the newcomers. "How grievous a thing it is that they should, by any means, be so abused as all those are, whom the Spaniards have any command or power over," *The World Encompassed* records Drake as saying; he hoped the English would establish a more noble legacy in the New World.

The *Golden Hind* sailed on northward, with Drake still hopeful of reuniting with the *Marigold* and the *Elizabeth*. A rendezvous had been set for 30 degrees south should the fleet be separated, and Drake did not want to believe that his companion vessels had sunk or deserted. But their failure to reappear deterred him from his intentions not at all, and over the months to come he cheerfully harried and looted Spain's small, undefended Pacific outposts in his single ship with virtual impunity. At the fishing port of Valparaiso, for example, the crew of a merchant ship in the harbor assumed that the *Golden Hind* was a fellow Spanish vessel, since foreign ships had never before braved those waters. The crew invited the newcomers aboard for wine and conversation, and the raiding party happily secured control of the ship and its cargo of gold, wine, and foodstuffs without a shot being fired. Since Drake's swift *Golden Hind* easily outran the warning of his arrival carried after him by slower Spanish merchant vessels, the pirates enjoyed similarly success at a half dozen other locations. "You will say this man who steals by day and prays by night in public is a devil," Drake said to one of his captives (religious services, as well as music, always accompanied Drake's evening meal), but for the most part the pirate treated his prisoners with the utmost graciousness, and they were rarely harmed. His quarrel was with King Philip and the perfidious Enríquez, he explained to them, and he bore individual Spaniards no animosity. Those prisoners who wrote accounts of their time with Drake noted the precision with which his men followed orders, the respect and affection the crew felt towards their commander, and the refinement, good manners, and good cheer of their captor, who delighted in music and spent his little free time painting pictures of the wildlife and landscapes—"birds, trees and sea-lions," according to da Silva—he had seen in the course of the voyage.

At Callao, Peru, in February 1579, Drake learned that the great prize he had been seeking—a treasure ship, fully laden with the silver from the Potosí mines and bound for Panama—had sailed just ahead of his arrival. The English set out in pursuit, cutting adrift all 30 of the ships anchored in the Callao harbor as they left. Just after crossing the equator on the afternoon of March 1, 1579, John Drake, the commander's young cousin, called out from the masthead. He had spied the sails of the *Nuestra Señora de la Concepción*, the Spanish treasure ship, and thus laid claim to the gold chain Drake had offered as a reward.

As word of the presence in the Pacific of the infernal Drake had not reached Callao before the treasure ship's departure, its captain, San Juan de Anton, slowed his vessel to allow the *Golden Hind* to come up alongside. Realization of the danger his ship was in dawned on the Spaniard too late; his refusal of Drake's command to surrender brought a volley of chain shot from the *Golden Hind*'s cannons that cut his mizzenmast, and the English swarmed aboard. Dressed in armored chain mail and a battle helmet, Drake joined him on the deck of the captured ship. "Accept with patience what is the usage of war," the pirate counseled as he placed his arm on the stunned captain's shoulder.

The English took more than a dozen large treasure chests of silver coins, some assorted jewels and pearls, 80 pounds of gold, and an incredible 26 tons of silver bullion from *Nuestra Señora*. The value of this haul is difficult to estimate, but its equivalent in English pounds of the day was more than half of the Crown's annual income and would be worth many millions of contemporary dollars. With this single prize, Drake had provided his investors with a greater return than any would have dared imagine and made himself one of England's wealthiest men.

After a week, Drake turned Captain Anton and his plundered ship free, leaving the Spanish with gifts and mementos—coins, pistols, a German musket, a silver basin engraved with the name Francisqus Drake—as consolation for their loss. He also left with them a letter addressed to the captains of the *Elizabeth* and *Marigold*, should they prove to be still in the Pacific. In it he asked them to treat Captain Anton fairly and without violence and promised to repay them for whatever costs might result from their encounter. The letter was signed, "Your sorrowful captain, whose heart is heavy for you, Francis Drake."

The pirates continued north, seeking a safe harbor in which to refit their hard-used vessel. Off the coast of present-day Nicaragua, Drake captured two more Spanish ships, both of them valuable prizes. From one he took charts of the rarely traveled transpacific trade route to the Philippines, intelligence that Spain regarded as one of its foremost state secrets; from the other, the ship of Don Francisco de Zarate, he took four chests of invaluable Chinese porcelains, linens, taffetas, and silks. (Mistakenly believing Zarate to be related to Enríquez, Drake initially threatened to hang him. "I would be more pleased to fall in with him [Enríquez]," Drake told Zarate, "than with all the silver and gold in the Indies, and [then] you would see how to comply with the word of a gentleman.") Then it was on to Gualtulco, a small Spanish settlement on the Gulf of Tehuantepec, in Mexico, where the English seized a ship in the harbor and then ransacked the town for the supplies they needed for their return voyage while, over a bottle of exquisite Spanish wine on the *Golden Hind*, Drake chatted with the town's captive dignitaries and let it be known that from their village he was off to Acapulco, which he intended to burn to the ground.

By the time Drake left Gualtulco, word of his presence had spread throughout Spanish America. Three ships and a militia were dispatched to the rescue of Acapulco. A small fleet was readied in the West Indies, should Drake attempt to return to England by crossing the Isthmus of Panama and seize shipping in the Caribbean, and preparations were made to guard the Strait of Magellan. But Drake had no intention of sailing in any of these waters; the threat against Acapulco was a ruse designed to secure his escape. Da Silva, the captive Portuguese pilot whom Drake had put ashore with his other prisoners at Gualtulco, believed that he knew the route the corsair would use for his getaway. "I think he will go on following the coast in search of the Strait, and when he does not find it will go home by way of China," da Silva accurately predicted to the Spanish authorities in Mexico.

The Portuguese was referring to another one of Dee's geographical theories, the so-called Strait of Anian. Along with other cosmographers, Dee posited the existence of a waterway across North America—the northern hemisphere's counterpart to the Strait of Magellan—that

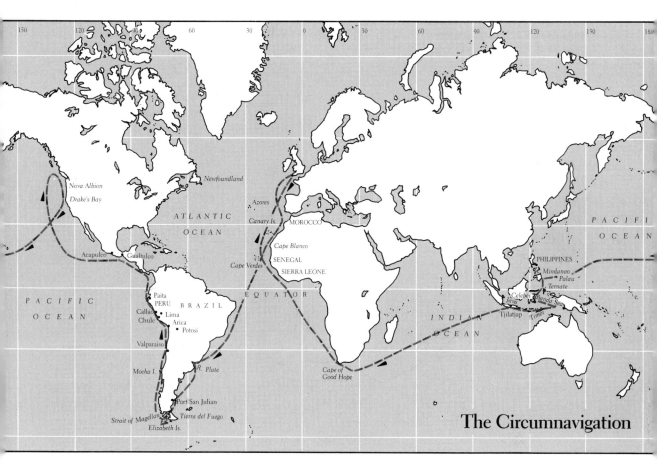

The Circumnavigation

would likewise link the Atlantic and Pacific oceans. It was generally believed that the Pacific opening to the Strait of Anian would be found in the unexplored northern latitudes near present-day Oregon and Washington, and it was for these uncharted waters that Drake, as da Silva had foreseen, now set sail.

The *Golden Hind* stood out due west from Mexico for almost 1,500 miles before changing course to the north. For weeks the indomitable little ship made good speed in fair winds and weather on the open sea, carrying its crew into waters rarely sailed by Europeans, but when the ship crossed 42 degrees north latitude (due west of the present-day border between the states of California and Oregon)

This Theodor de Bry engraving portrays Drake and his men encountering the Native Americans at what he called Nova Albion. The English landfall was probably somewhere in the vicinity of San Francisco Bay.

in early June, the weather changed for the worse. Icy winds, hail, and freezing fog beset the overloaded *Golden Hind*. Hoping to outlast the freakish weather, Drake held his course steadily north until 48 degrees north latitude, where at last he anchored in an open bay. Had Dee's theories been correct, the coastline would have begun falling away to the east at about 40 degrees north; instead, as Drake observed, the coast trended to the northwest, and, of course, there was no opening for the strait.

The *Golden Hind* was now leaky and battered, and Drake, having been forced to abandon his plan of returning to England through North America, took the ship south again in search of a sheltered harbor where he and his men could perform the necessary repairs. Hugging the shoreline as a precaution in case the perilous condition of his ship forced it to be unloaded, Drake took the *Golden Hind* some 700 miles south along an "unhandsome and deformed" (Fletcher's words) coast, to, on June 17, a landing in the vicinity of what is known today as San Francisco Bay. There, before the amazed eyes of the native Miwok Indians, the *Golden Hind* was raised out of the water onto a wooden scaffold, and its cracked or rotting timbers were replaced, its joints were completely recaulked, and its sails and rigging were repaired. A small stockade was built and a forge set up, where the work of the ship's blacksmith in fashioning new chains and braces fascinated the Miwoks. "They came down unto us," reads the account in *The World Encompassed*, "and yet with no hostile meaning or intent to hurt us; standing, when they drew near, as men ravished in their minds, with the sight of such things as they never had seen or heard of before that time: their errand being rather with submission and fear to worship us as gods, than to have any war with us as mortal men." Modern scholars believe that the Miwoks probably regarded the newcomers as the ghosts of their deceased ancestors rather than as gods; Drake chose to interpret the peacefulness displayed by the Miwoks as "submission and fear" and an invitation

(continued on page 81)

The Invincible Armada

A 17th-century map showing the route of the Armada up the English Channel and its ignominious retreat around Scotland and Ireland.

The English often like to cast their country's fateful encounter with Spain's so-called Invincible Armada (detailed in Chapter Six) as a David and Goliath struggle in which virtues subsequently regarded as quintessentially British—pluck, perseverance, and an understated, imperturbable resolution—enabled the island nation to triumph over insurmountable odds. The showdown between Philip's massive fleet and Elizabeth's determined defenders of the realm is rightly seen as a turning point in English history—the beginning of the long, slow demise of imperial Spain and England's corresponding ascent to world power—and, like the legend of Drake's drum, has served the English people as inspiration at times when their nation has again been threatened by foreign might, such as during the Battle of Britain and the evacuation of Dunkirk in World War II. But though perhaps only Drake and a few of his fellow seamen were truly confident of victory when the Armada was sighted off the southwest tip of England in the summer of 1588, the advantages in the ensuing struggle were not nearly as one-sided in favor of Spain as commonly assumed. Spain's fleet outnumbered England's, true, and its individual ships were generally larger than their English counterparts, but Drake and his cohorts were much more expert than the Spanish captains in maneuvering their nimbler vessels and possessed as well a greater understanding of gunnery tactics, whereas the outdated Spanish strategy hinged still on hand-to-hand fighting across the heaving decks of two ships bound with grappling hooks. In the end, of course, the advantage was all to the English, as, for much of the next three centuries, it would be everywhere on the waters that carried England's mariners to the far-flung regions they would claim as their nation's dominion.

Queen Elizabeth I, pictured with the victorious
English and the storm-tossed Spanish fleets behind
her. The queen's steadfastness was a great consolation to her people during the crisis with Spain.
"Let tyrants fear," she proclaimed before her troops
at Tilbury while the Armada was menacing England.
"I have always so behaved myself that, under God,
I have placed my chiefest strength and safeguard in
the loyal hearts and good will of my subjects."

None of Elizabeth's subjects had a more
loyal heart or bore her more good will than
Sir Francis Drake, seen here in one of the
many likenesses of him rendered after the
English defeat of the Armada. In the aftermath of the English victory, Drake became
one of the most famous men in Europe.
Even Pope Sixtus V, who had contributed
financially to the Armada, was impressed.
"Have you heard how Drake with his fleet
has offered battle to the Armada?" said the
pontiff. "With what courage! Do you think
he showed any fear? He is a great captain!"

With the Spanish fleet in flames in the distance, Elizabeth, riding her famous white gelding, reviews her troops at Tilbury. "Therefore I am come amongst you at this time, not as for my recreation or sport, but being resolved in the midst and heat of the battle, to live and die amongst you all; to lay down for my God, and for my kingdom and for my people, my honour and my blood even in the dust," she proclaimed.

The ships of the English fleet were generally smaller, swifter, better armed, and more maneuverable than the sluggish Spanish warships, which were designed primarily to carry a great number of soldiers. According to the historian John Sugden, the English ships "heralded a new and revolutionary mode of naval warfare. The ship should not be a mere transport, loaded with men. . . . It was itself an agent of destruction."

This map shows the Spanish Armada in its nearly invincible crescent formation. Recognizing that they could not break the formation head-on—"We durst not adventure to put in among them, their fleet being so strong," Lord Howard advised Lord Walsingham—the English maneuvered their ships behind the crescent in the dead of night and attacked from both sides.

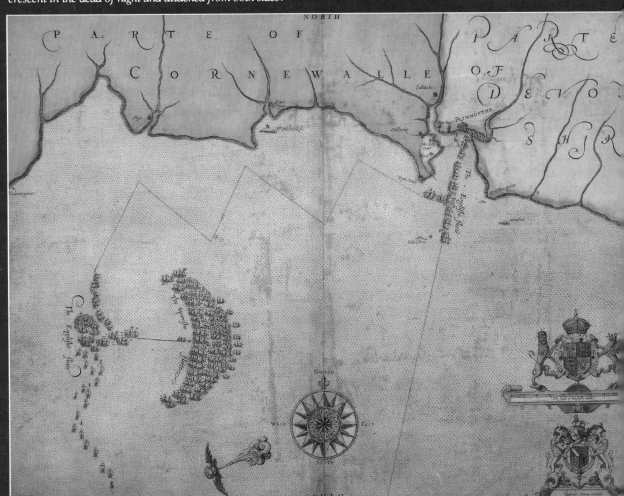

The defeat of his Armada left King Philip II of Spain broken in spirit. "If God does not send us a miracle," he said as the first reports of the disaster began to reach his kingdom in the autumn of 1588, "I hope to die and go to Him . . . so as not to see so much ill fortune and disgrace." He descended thereafter into a solitary melancholia, which was lifted briefly with the announcement of Drake's death in 1596. "It is good news," said the Spanish monarch then, "and now I will get well."

Drake, pictured here, little knew how his exploits would affect England's naval history and the face of the globe. Though the English would use their naval superiority—born with Drake's escapades—to claim an empire that would ultimately cover one-fifth of the earth's land and include one-fourth of the world's population, the patriotic sea dog regretted that he had not done even more for his country: "If I have not performed as much as was looked for, yet I persuade myself that his good Lordship will confess that I have been dutiful," he wrote.

(continued from page 72)

to take their "province and kingdom into his hand, and become their king and patron." In the name of "her majesty Queen Elizabeth and her successors forever," Drake then claimed the land, which he called Nova Albion (*Nova* meaning "new"; *Albion* being a Roman name for England), and raised a post bearing a brass plaque to that effect.

Drake and the English stayed at the California bay a full five weeks, exploring the inland's lush, wildlife-filled forests as well as several Miwok villages, where the Indians lived in distinctive, earth-covered conical huts with exceptional heat-conserving properties. Their friendship with the Miwoks was enhanced by Drake's attempts to tend some of their illnesses and injuries with the few medical supplies and techniques he could offer—"lotions, plasters, and ointments according to the state of their griefs." When the *Golden Hind*, reprovisioned and repaired, set sail on July 23, 1579, the Miwoks showed much sorrow "with bitter tears and wringing of their hands tormenting themselves." As the ship put out to sea, the Indians clambered up mountain paths to light signal fires at the crests of their protected bay's encircling hills, trying to keep it in sight.

The piratical explorers were now committed to returning home by circumnavigating the globe, and Drake set a southwesterly course for the Spice Islands and the Far East. For the next 68 days the *Golden Hind* was alone on the open Pacific, where Magellan and those others who had attempted to circle the world had suffered such unspeakable horrors of hunger and disease. Favorable winds often powered the little ship more than 100 miles per day, but even the most up-to-date charts of the Pacific that Drake had liberated from Spanish ships underrepresented the actual 7,000-mile distance they would sail before sighting land again in the form of one of the Caroline Islands. The natives who paddled out in dugout canoes to meet the sailing ship appeared friendly, but they soon began swarming over the sides, climbing up the rigging, fighting among themselves over the trinkets the English offered them, and pilfering anything they could make away with. A warning shot fired by the *Golden Hind*'s guns only increased the tumult and sparked an attack by the natives, and Drake ordered the guns to be turned on them, resulting in great loss of life.

In hope of avoiding further incidents, Drake proceeded conservatively for the next few weeks, refusing to put in for more than brief rewatering stops. He took the *Golden Hind* through poorly charted waters off the green, jungle-clad coasts of the Philippine archipelago and navigated the Siau Passage with the aide of native pilots. On November 3, his ship entered the Molucca Sea, and he and his crew sighted the fabled Spice Islands, whose wealth rivaled that of Spain's holdings in the New World.

Spices, particularly pepper and cloves, were literally worth their weight in gold in Europe, where they were used as flavor enhancers, food preservatives, perfumes, and medicines. Portugal's 16th-century monopoly over the few parts of the world where these precious items grew in pungent abundance—the Moluccas and the Sunda Isles and the coastal islands off eastern Africa—had therefore made it one of the wealthiest nations in Europe. Drake arrived in the Moluccas at a time of great unrest. Babu, the sultan of Ternate (the northernmost of the Moluccas), who controlled the bulk of the clove trade in the region, was engaged in an effort to rid his islands of the Portuguese, who had murdered his father six years earlier, and he welcomed the opportunity to recruit the English to his cause.

Babu therefore welcomed the *Golden Hind* and its men to the port of Talangam with a display of the opulence for which his ancient kingdom was celebrated. Four ornately decorated war barges, each manned by 80 oarsmen and a phalanx of ceremonial officers and armed militia, rowed out to meet the English ship and guide it to anchor. Babu himself followed in the royal vessel, a tall, handsome man adorned in "cloth of gold," red leather shoes, gold or-

Drake and the English arrive at the court of Babu, sultan of Ternate. "Captain Francis went to the fortress of Ternate," wrote a Spanish emissary to the Moluccas. "The King of Ternate soon opened negotiations with him, saying that he was not a friend of the Portuguese but an independent king. . . . Captain Francis . . . promised that within two years he would decorate that sea with ships for whatever purpose might be necessary."

naments and chains, and turquoise, emerald, ruby, and diamond rings; so magnificent was the sultan that Drake called out his musicians and trumpeters to play their instruments on deck as he approached. Babu then invited the master mariner to stay and parley with him in a captured Portuguese castle of great splendor.

Within three days, Drake struck an agreement with the sultan that would please Queen Elizabeth even more than the colony in North America. Babu willingly granted England exclusive rights to trade in all his islands in exchange for Elizabeth's promise of naval help. In recognition of the new relationship between his kingdom and England, the sultan made Drake a gift of six tons of cloves—as much as could be stowed in the *Golden Hind*'s already straining holds—and sent Queen Elizabeth a beautiful ring.

From Ternate, Drake made for the Banda Sea, where, somewhere east of Celebes, he overhauled the *Golden Hind* yet again on a deserted but beautiful island and made plans for the upcoming voyage through the Indian Ocean to Africa's Cape of Good Hope.

With no pilots to guide him nor charts in any language to suggest what landforms to avoid, Drake guided his ship through a maze of islands, coral reefs, and stony peninsulas "with extraordinary care and circumspection." Weeks passed. Contrary winds drove the *Golden Hind* south when Drake wanted to head west, and he had to sail below Celebes rather than pass to its north.

On the evening of January 9, 1580, the English were sailing somewhere near two degrees south latitude in what seemed to be open sea, "at which time we supposed that we had at last attained a free passage." A fair wind blew and "followed us as we desired with a reasonable gale," and Drake ordered all sails drawn out for full speed. Suddenly, "when we least suspected, no show or suspicion of danger appearing to us," a tremendous jolt shook the *Golden Hind* from stem to stern. The dreadful sound of timbers splintering was heard as the ship crashed to a dead halt, "laid up

This portrayal of the Golden Hind *foundering on the reef off Celebes was a detail in a French world map engraved by Nicola Van Sype in 1583. The Van Sype map was one of the first to show the new possessions—the Elizabeth Islands and Nova Albion— that Drake had claimed for England.*

THE WORLD
Encompassed
By
Sir FRANCIS DRAKE,

Being his next voyage to that to *Nombre*
de Dios formerly imprinted;

Carefully collected out of the notes of Master
FRANCIS FLETCHER *Preacher in this im-
ployment, and divers others his followers in
the same* :

Offered now at last to publique view, both for the honour of
the actor, but especially for the stirring vp of *heroick spirits,*
to benefit their Countrie, and eternize their names
by like noble attempts.

LONDON,
Printed for NICHOLAS BOVRNE
and are to be sold at his shop at the

*The title page of the original
edition of* The World Encompassed. *The book relies on the
narrative of Francis Fletcher and
"diverse" others and was published at the instigation of Drake's
nephew Francis Drake in 1628,
though it was probably compiled
decades earlier, perhaps with the
involvement of the master mariner
himself.*

fast upon a desperate shoal," according to *The World Encompassed*. The vessel had run up on an undersea reef, and
water rushed into its hull while the wind still filling the
sails ground the *Golden Hind* ever more firmly against the
submerged rock.

As night set in, panic and despair threatened to over-
whelm the crew. "Notwithstanding that we expected
nothing but imminent death," Drake, whose faith rarely
faltered, led his men in a prayer for deliverance and then
"encouraged us all to bestir ourselves, showing us the way
thereto by his own example" as he set them to pump the
holds so that the damage could be inspected and repairs
could be effected. Miraculously, the steady wind that forced
it further aground also prevented the *Golden Hind* from
heeling over and sinking. Working without pause through
the night and into the next day, the crew managed to keep
the incoming waters at bay. The damage, they found, might
possibly be repaired if the ship could be floated off the reef.
Spurred on by that hope, Drake ordered tons of cloves,
provisions, ammunition, and artillery jettisoned to lighten
the load; "nor even those things which we before this time
never could be without . . . could find favor with us, but
everything as it first came to hand went overboard."

On the afternoon of January 10, after repeated attempts
to free the *Golden Hind* had failed "and left us nothing to
trust to but prayers and tears," a shift in the wind accomplished what all the Englishmen's desperate efforts
could not: the *Golden Hind* teetered precariously toward its
damaged side, then wallowed upright, slipped off the reef,
"and by that means . . . made us glad men." The damaged
ship limped eastward through equally dangerous waters for
another month until Drake found an anchorage off an
unnamed island where repairs could be made. The durable
double-sheathed oak hull that Drake had insisted upon had
saved his expedition; a single layer of planking would not
have withstood the impact of the crash.

Made ready again, the *Golden Hind* slipped westward and
southward, steering clear of ports or shipping ways known

to the Portuguese. Drake sailed carefully along the south coast of the island of Java, becoming the first European to navigate those waters and thereby proving that Java was not, as some believed, part of Terra Australis. At Tjilatjap, on the island's southern coast, the weary mariners took on fresh water and other provisions and made ready to cross the Indian Ocean. For two months the *Golden Hind* sailed uneventfully on the south equatorial current, out of sight of land or another sail, until on May 21 its crew at last spied the southeastern coast of Africa at 31.5 degrees south latitude. The various narrative accounts of the journey say little of these last months, making mention only of the explorers' anxious search for fresh water as the ship rounded the Cape of Good Hope in June. By the time the 58 surviving sailors made land at Sierra Leone on the Guinea Coast of West Africa in late July, water rations had been cut to a half pint a day for every three men.

The silence of the journals regarding the penultimate leg of the *Golden Hind*'s extraordinary voyage should not detract from the magnitude of Drake's achievement, for from Java he had safely guided his ship an extraordinary 9,700 miles without stopping and without accurate charts, by far the longest open-sea voyage made by a European to that time—an astonishing feat that a prominent 18th-cenury naval historian rightly deemed "a thing hardly to be credited." A few days more than two months after the Sierra Leone landfall, the *Golden Hind* sailed once again into the calm waters of her home port of Plymouth, "the place of our first setting forth, after we had spent 2 years, 10 months, and some odd days beside in seeing the wonders of our Lord in the deep." The first English voyage on the Pacific, Indian, or South Atlantic oceans was complete, and Francis Drake had become the first captain in history to sail his own ship around the world.

The Wind Commands Me Away

The Plymouth homecoming marked the end of Drake's career as an explorer. Though he would never again sail unknown seas or discover new lands, the last 15 years of his life were as action filled as the first 40 had been and in many respects even more glorious, for the successful voyage of the *Golden Hind* ushered in a new era both for himself and for England.

During Drake's almost three-year absence, the bits of news concerning his adventures and exploits that infrequently reached England spawned fascination, confusion, and ire. The return of John Winter and the *Elizabeth* in mid-1579 with its half-starved crew's tale of their harrowing passage through the Strait of Magellan fed rumors that the expedition had failed, and Winter, an unlucky scapegoat, found himself imprisoned in London on piracy charges intended to assuage Spain's outrage, a fate many assumed Drake would share should he return to England safely. Philip, the recipient of a steady stream of correspondence detailing "the boldness of this low man" in plundering Spanish colonies and vessels, filed an angry claim with Queen Elizabeth for the restitution of all Drake had stolen. The Spanish king still stopped short of overt reprisals against English shipping or commerce, but Drake's offenses certainly raised the level of hostility between the two nations.

Drake put much thought into his coat of arms, symbol of his accession to gentility. Shown here is the coat of arms assigned him by Queen Elizabeth, with which Drake was unhappy because he claimed that it omitted the ancient family crest of the Drakes, a red-winged dragon. The stars above and below the undulating line on the shield were silver and were intended to symbolize the North and South poles; the crest assigned him by Elizabeth is a knight's helmet surmounted by a globe on which rides a sailing ship.

Once the *Golden Hind* had at last reanchored in Plymouth Harbor, the usually cautious Elizabeth's decision to receive Drake as a hero and bestow upon him the ultimate honor of knighthood exacerbated the tension, as did her manipulation of the freebooted treasure. The 4,700 percent profit later boasted of by Drake's investors suggest that his apportionment of the shares the queen allowed him to remove from the Tower of London before the formal tally of the treasure was very generous. His high-seas adventuring ultimately left Drake not only the most famous man in Europe—he sat for several portraits, copies of which circulated widely on the Continent, and his likeness adorned everything from dishes to playing cards—but one of the wealthiest men in England. "Drake is squandering more money than any man in England," the Spanish ambassador Mendoza indignantly reported to Philip and then went on to list the lavish gifts the pirate was bestowing on Elizabeth and her councillors, most of them—an emerald crown, a diamond cross, gold bars—originating in Spain or its colonies.

Drake's achievements inspired numerous English schemes for further exploration and overseas commerce. Mendoza complained to his king that "at present there is hardly an Englishman who is not talking of undertaking the voyage, so encouraged are they by Drake's return." Though virtually all of these ventures failed, Drake's success left Elizabeth and her advisers committed to the rapid development of England's navy and maritime enterprises, which they saw as the nation's shortest course to obtaining its own empire. In 1583, Drake—along with Sir Walter Raleigh, Sir Martin Frobisher, and England's other great captains—was named to a new Royal Commission on the Navy, which was charged with overseeing the reform of naval practices, the rapid construction of high-tonnage ships, and the overall development of the navy as England's best weapon against hostile powers, particularly Spain.

Between 1580 and 1585, Drake engaged vigorously in public life. He became mayor of Plymouth and a member

Elizabeth Sydenham, Drake's second wife, as she appeared in 1583, two years before her marriage to the most famous man in England. Drake's new wife was herself the heiress of one of the wealthiest and most distinguished men in the West Country.

of the House of Commons. He acquired several properties that befit his new status as a knight and a member of the gentry, foremost among them his "gentleman's estate" of Buckland Abbey, a grandly appointed former monastery in the countryside between Plymouth and Tavistock. After the unexpected death of his first wife, Mary, in 1583, he married a young noblewoman, Elizabeth Sydenham, further securing his place in society.

But his personal war with Philip remained his obsession. When, at a social gathering one evening, the earl of Sussex suggested that it was no great feat to capture an unarmed treasure ship, Drake immediately retorted that he was ready to make war against the king of Spain himself. He ceaselessly promoted ideas for ventures against Spanish interests, such as directly attacking a flota, invading the Azores, or various schemes for placing Dom Antonio, a Portuguese claimant to his nation's crown, on the throne of Portugal, only to be restrained by Elizabeth.

This enforced inactivity (as regards Spain) ended in 1585 when, in reprisal for Elizabeth's support of the Dutch in the Netherlands, where an English army was soon to take the field, Philip seized English merchant ships that had called at Spanish ports on the Continent and used the equipment, supplies, and arms he stripped from them to outfit his own fleet. Drake received the queen's commission to liberate the impounded ships and crews, but the rescue mission was simply a ploy to disguise his true intent, for Philip had released the ships before his nemesis, in command of the largest "private" force mustered in England to date—some 29 ships and 2,300 men, including vessels from the queen's navy and soldiers from her army—ever set sail. Drake's actual destination, after attacks made on the Cape Verde Islands and the Canary Islands en route, was once again the West Indies.

Despite the death of 300 men from fever on the outward leg of the voyage, Drake arrived in the Caribbean with a formidable force at his command. His first target was Santo Domingo, on the island of Hispaniola, Spain's oldest city

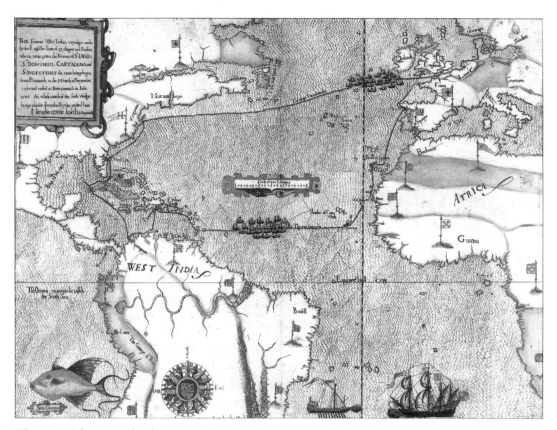

This map of the route taken by
Drake's ships in the course of his
1585–86 raid on the Spanish cities
of the New World was drawn by
Baptista Boazio and appeared in
Walter Bigges's Summary and
True Discourse of Sir Francis
Drake's West India Voyage,
the first full-length account of one
of Drake's voyages to appear in
print. Its simultaneous publication
in London, Leyden, and Cologne
in 1589 attests to Drake's fame
on the Continent as well as in
England. Bigges was a captain
in Drake's fleet.

in the Americas and the administrative capital of the
Spanish Main. A carefully coordinated, simultaneous attack by land and sea brought the fall of the terrified city in
a day; most of the populace, when they learned that it was
the dreaded "El Draque" who had arrived in their harbor
on the first day of the new year 1586, fled to the hinter-
lands. For the next month, the English plundered and
burned the city, devoting special attention to the cathedral
and other houses of worship, until its magistrates and
officials were at last able to raise the ransom that Drake
demanded.

The desecration of their churches and the hanging of two
Dominican friars at Drake's orders reinforced the Spanish
image of him as a demonic heretic. "Nothing remains but
life itself," wrote a sad city official to Philip, though one of

those who negotiated the ransom with Drake found him less than monstrous, perhaps recognizing that in sparing most of Santo Domingo's residents, the celebrated English seaman had been more generous than many another conqueror of the day would have been. This individual described Drake as "sharp, restless, well-spoken, inclined to liberality and to ambition, vainglorious, boastful," a "man of medium stature . . . rather heavy than slender, merry, careful" who "commands and governs imperiously . . . is feared and obeyed by his men" and "punishes resolutely," though he was in sum, thought the observer, "not very cruel."

Next was Cartagena, which, despite the protection of a natural double harbor and exceptionally well-engineered fortifications built into rock cliffsides, capitulated to Drake after a surprise attack by land and sea in early February and less than a day's heavy fighting. Six weeks of negotiation, supplemented by arson and looting, yielded a ransom, although the overall take, as at Santo Domingo, was again less than Drake had hoped. Determined to bring home enough treasure to pay off his backers, he then laid plans for an attack on the city of Panama, but an epidemic of malaria among his crew forced him to reconsider, and the fleet set its course for home via the southeast coast of North America. The English destroyed St. Augustine, a Spanish settlement and fortress on the Atlantic coast in the northern part of the Florida peninsula, before calling at Roanoke Island, off the coast of present-day North Carolina, where under the direction of Sir Walter Raleigh the first English colony in North America had been established the previous year. The settlement was struggling, however; the expected supply ships from England had not arrived, and the colonists were ready to abandon the venture. Drake agreed to carry them back to England, where his ships docked at Portsmouth in late July 1586.

Though disappointing financially, Drake's voyage had been a major strategic success. It demonstrated a pre-

viously unsuspected weakness in Philip's empire to Spain's
enemies, lifted England's confidence, damaged Spain's morale, and greatly aggravated Philip's ongoing financial
problems. The Spanish king had debts to match the enor-
mous income provided him by the New World's gold and
silver. His predecessor, Charles I, had borrowed ex-
travagantly from foreign bankers to secure his election as
the Holy Roman Emperor, a practice Philip continued in
order to arm and outfit his armies. Alarmed by the vulnerability of Philip's farflung dominions that Drake had
demonstrated and the rise in attacks on Spanish shipping that he inspired—piracy became a virtual industry in
England, where, according to Spain's ambassador, "every
gentleman buildeth a ship or two to send after Sir Francis
Drake"—Philip's bankers tightened their credit. Spain's
merchant community railed against England, for not only
the New World trade but also the all-important commerce
with the Netherlands—Spain's only access to which was
by the English Channel—was imperiled by the audacity of
Drake and his imitators.

"Truly, Sir Francis Drake is a fearful man to the king of
Spain," wrote Burghley, and Philip determined to rid himself of the menace posed by this rabid sea dog and others of
his kind. In 1586, following Drake's return, the Spanish
monarch began planning what he called the "Enterprise of
England"—an invasion of the island nation for the purpose
of placing himself upon its throne and returning it to
Catholicism. (This last prospect appealed greatly to the
pope, who pledged one million crowns toward Philip's
project.) The centerpiece of his strategy was the formation
of an armada, or armed naval fleet, that was to be the largest
and strongest ever assembled. The Spanish Armada was to
be used to take control of the English Channel, across
which Philip's army in the Netherlands would be ferried to
invade England.

As reports of Philip's preparations reached England in the
winter months of 1586–87, Drake was adamant in his

advice to Elizabeth: strike at Spain first, before the Armada became a genuine threat. Ever cautious, Elizabeth hesitated, but in March 1587 Drake convinced her to sign a new commission for him. He was to hit at Philip's concentrated areas of preparation, "impeach the provisions of Spain," and otherwise make himself a hindrance to the Enterprise of England. By early April, Drake, worried that the queen might change her mind and order him not to enter Spanish ports, had 24 ships and almost 3,000 men under sail. "The wind commands me away," he wrote to Walsingham in announcing his departure.

Drake's second campaign as an admiral at war revealed his developing genius for military strategy; at war, as in piracy, he relied on surprise and daring. His first encounter

The Spanish Armada masses in the harbor of Cádiz prior to Drake's daring raid on that port in April 1587. "Give me a fleet and a free hand and I will smoke the wasps out of their nests," Drake said to Elizabeth in arguing for a preemptive strike on the Spanish. An eyewitness described the destruction that Drake visited upon vessels at Cádiz: "With the pitch and tar they had, smoke and flames rose up, so that it seemed like a huge volcano, or something out of Hell . . . a sad and dreadful sight."

with Spanish forces in European waters took place at Cádiz. Overriding the objections of his principal officers, who urged a more cautious approach, Drake led his ships right into Cádiz harbor, which was a center of Armada preparation, in broad daylight and captured, burned, or sank 30 Spanish vessels. Within the city itself, news of Drake's arrival caused such a panic that 26 people were trampled to death in the citizenry's frenzied rush to safety in Cádiz castle. The impact on Spanish morale of Drake's raid was immense, for, as an eyewitness put it, "the nonchalance that there was was so great and the confidence that no enemy would dare to enter the bay, as they were so little accustomed to see seagoing ships dare to do so, nor had it been heard in many centuries previous of any having such daring to break through the gates and entrances of their port." Though Drake delighted in his feat—"he had singed the king of Spain's beard," he said—he harbored no illusions that he had dealt the Armada a death blow, and the obvious magnitude of Philip's enterprise impressed him. "I dare not almost write unto your honour of the great forces we hear the King of Spain hath out in the Straits," he warned Walsingham by letter. "Prepare in England strongly, and most by sea. Stop him now, and stop him ever!"

From Cádiz, Drake took his fleet northwest to Cape St. Vincent, the headland at the extreme southwestern tip of the Iberian Peninsula. Once again, his strategy upset his chief officers, whose counsel he had not sought. They protested to him that they had been made simply "witnesses to the words you have delivered" and attempted to dissuade him from his assault on the cape; he ignored their advice, and by early May his forces had overrun both Cape St. Vincent and the nearby town of Sagres. A hundred or more Spanish vessels and a huge quantity of timber and other useful materials and supplies were burned, and the English enjoyed themselves immensely in Catholic houses of worship and religious contemplation: "The nefarious English entered the holy convent," wrote an eyewitness;

"they carried out their customary banquets and drunken revelry, their diabolic extravagances and obscenities; they stole all they could get their hands on and set fire to the place. Likewise, they carried out a thousand acts of contempt and profanities on the images of the saints, like unadulterated heretics; because, just as darkness is offended by light, so these infernal people abhor radiant brightness."

A satisfied Drake then made for the Portuguese capital city of Lisbon, where much of the Armada was assembling, and succeeded in blockading the harbor for several days, serving notice to Europe that the balance of power was changing. "The English are masters of the sea, and hold it at their discretion," wrote Venice's ambassador to Spain. "Lisbon and the whole coast is, as it were, blockaded."

Then, as suddenly as he had appeared, Drake was gone. By June, he was off the Azores in hope of intercepting a flota from the Spanish Main. Instead he came across the single richest prize of his life, a huge carrack belonging to the Portuguese king that carried a double cargo of spices, fabrics, woods, jewels, porcelain, silver, and gold from the East Indies. The *San Felipe* was so large that Drake managed to take it only by sailing his nine small English ships up against its fortresslike hull and holding fast below the level of its many guns while firing down into the great ship's holds. The haul from the *San Felipe* more than repaid the expenses of Drake's expedition and, by diverting Philip's fleet into pursuit of him, delayed the assembly of the Armada for months.

Determined to bring the heretical and troublesome island nation under control of Catholic power at any cost, the exasperated Philip finally dispatched the Armada on its Enterprise of England on May 20, 1588. Drake's raids on Iberian ports had served their purpose: Philip had been forced to set back his fleet's launch date for a full year while England built up its own naval resources and fortified its defenses in the English Channel. Even so, when the Spanish Armada at last set sail it proudly bore the title of

The signature of Francis Drake is the third one affixed in the left-hand column, just above that of John Hawkins, of these minutes of a council of war held aboard the flagship Ark Royal *by the commanding officers of the British fleet in 1588.*

"Invincible," and few other than Drake himself disputed the claim. It was the largest European fleet ever assembled; more than 130 ships under the command of the duke of Medina Sidonia, all heavily armed and generally much larger than their English counterparts, sailed with over 20,000 men toward an intended rendezvous with the duke of Parma's 30,000-strong army in the Netherlands, a large portion of which would then be carried over to England.

But Drake's foresight enabled England to prepare. "The advantage of time and place in all martial actions is half a victory," he wrote to Elizabeth in requesting command of a fleet of 50 ships to hold off the Spanish, and by spring of 1588 the English force was deployed in the Channel, although Drake had been bypassed for command in favor of the navy's lord admiral, Baron Howard of Effingham. In her wisdom, Elizabeth thought it better that overall command go to a born nobleman. On both his most recent attack on the West Indies and his raids on the Iberian ports, Drake had had severe disagreements with his noble officers, similar in kind if not in outcome to the dispute with Doughty. Within England, Drake's rapid rise, his fame, and his status as Elizabeth's favorite made him the object of much resentment, as did, on the seas, his impetuous command style. Knowing that she could rely on Drake's loyalty, Elizabeth believed that she could minimize dissension by entrusting Howard as her commander. Drake was named vice-admiral, second-in-command, and Howard, who had no experience of naval warfare, prudently relied on him for advice on tactics.

In the early months of 1588, before the Armada sailed, Drake, as always, advised attack, but foul weather and the hesitance of Elizabeth and her advisers held the English ships at Plymouth. Legend has it that Drake, who was aptly posted to the 450-ton *Revenge*, and Howard were spending the lovely afternoon of July 19 in a friendly game of bowling on the grassy flats overlooking Plymouth Sound when a messenger brought them the news that all England had been dreading for months: masses of gaudily painted and mightily armed Spanish warships had been sighted nearby. "We have time enough to finish the game and beat the Spaniards, too," Drake is said to have calmly advised Howard.

Upon first contact in the Channel, the men of both fleets became quickly aware of the advantages possessed by the other. Despite its inferiority in terms of number of vessels and manpower, the English fleet had the advantage of fighting in its home waters, where its captains knew each landform and underwater characteristic and were able to dart their smaller, faster, more maneuverable ships into nearby harbors to be resupplied. The English were also more adept gunners. In battle, the Spanish relied on positioning their ships so that the men aboard could board their enemy's vessels, a tactic that the ensuing battles would help demonstrate was becoming increasingly outmoded; gunnery was a secondary consideration. The English ships carried more and better guns, and their commanders intended to fight at a certain distance so that the weapons could do their work.

The Spanish sought to offset these English advantages and utilize their own strength through the sustained use of an almost impenetrable crescent formation. The crescent

According to one of the most famous Drake legends, he was nonchalantly loath to interrupt the game of bowling he was enjoying with Baron Howard when they received the news about the arrival of the Armada. (Seen here is a 19th-century painting of the bowling scene by Seymour Lucas.) This particular legend, as well as the one about Drake's drum, enjoyed its greatest popularity during World War II, when England was once again menaced by a foreign enemy.

The Spanish Armada enters the English Channel. The Spanish called their fleet the Invincible Armada; according to one observer it was "the greatest navy that ever swam upon the sea." King Philip believed that its victory was divinely ordained. "All victories are the gifts of God Almighty, and the cause we champion is so exclusively His, we may fairly look for His aid and favor," wrote the Spanish monarch.

led with its massive center, where Medina Sidonia stationed his own flagship, the *San Martín*, and his 24 battle galleons and galleasses. Supply ships followed the front battle line, backed by flanking wings of smaller warships. The English recognized immediately that without paying a heavy cost they could gain no clear entry into the formation, which proceeded up the Channel with stately, ominous precision.

Instead, under cover of night, Drake positioned the bulk of the British strength behind the Armada. Rain and wind worked against the clumsy Spanish ships as Howard sent his fastest, best-armed ships between the crescent's north wing and the English coast to protect Plymouth from attack and launched a two-sided assault against the Armada. Steady fighting throughout the first day's engagement, on

July 21, left both sides apprehensive, with neither clearly in control. While Elizabeth rallied her land forces with an inspirational speech at Tilbury—"I know I have the body of a weak and feeble woman, but I have the heart of a King, and of a King of England too, and think foul scorn that Parma or Spain, or any prince of Europe, should dare to invade the borders of my realms: to which, rather than any dishonour shall grow by me, I myself will take up arms," she told her cheering subjects—ragtag swarms of small fishing boats and private trading vessels, like the one Drake had captained after his adolescent apprenticeship, came out to support the English fleet in defense of their homeland.

Tactical errors, indecision, and foul weather hampered both sides as they proceeded up the Channel in a slow, deadly game of bull and matador; although neither fleet sustained much actual damage in these early days of the campaign, Drake and his *Revenge* managed to claim the munitions and treasure of a broken-masted galleon. Several confusing, inconclusive battles ended with the Spanish

Accompanied by the Roebuck and a pinnace, Drake and the Revenge *approach the* Nuestra Señora del Rosario, *whose broken masts and damaged rigging had caused it to become separated from the rest of the Armada. The* Rosario *was one of the largest and best-armed ships of the Spanish fleet, and it carried one-third of the money to be used by the Armada, as Drake discovered after its capture.*

The Ships of Andeluzia, Comanded by Don Pedro Valdes which were 10 Galleons, 1 Pinace having in them 2400 Souldiers 800 Mariners, 260 Canons.&

Spanish Armada playing cards were an extremely popular item in England following the defeat of the invincible fleet; all the knaves in the deck featured a Catholic clergyman. "The invincible and dreadful navy, with all its great and terrible ostentation, did not in all their sailing about England so much as sink or take one ship, bark, pinnace or cockboat of ours, or even burn so much as one sheepcote on this land," an exuberant Drake was quoted as saying.

reforming and refining their crescent but never daring to try the strategic ports Drake and Howard were determined to protect. On July 28, with the Spanish off Calais, France, Howard authorized Drake to send "hell-burner" fire ships—hulks drenched with gunpowder, pitch, resin-soaked rags, anything flammable—into the midst of the Armada. At midnight, as eight blazing fire ships drifted infernally among the clustered galleons, the Spanish discipline shattered and the crescent dissolved. In the morning, the newly reinforced English fleet, now numbering almost 150 vessels, punished the disorganized Spanish, who lost at least 1,500 men that day alone. In the aftermath of the Battle of Gravelines, as the English called the decisive encounter, winds and Drake chased the Spanish into the North Sea, away from the planned rendezvous with Parma. Daring not retry the Channel, the defeated Armada made its return to Spain by sailing north and west around Scotland and Ireland, where several ships were wrecked on the wild, stony coasts. Nearly half of Philip's fleet was lost to battle or shipwreck before it returned to Spain; 15,000 men were killed or captured. The English lost not a single ship and less than 100 men. "I have read it all, although I would rather not have done, because it hurts so much," commented Philip after receiving a report of the disaster.

Drake emerged as the most widely hailed hero of the campaign, but he was unwilling to rest. Having humbled Philip, he now wished to humiliate him. When Dom Antonio, the Portuguese pretender, proposed a new scheme that would restore him to the throne, Drake became an enthusiastic proponent. In exchange for an English military invasion of Portugal—his people, he claimed, would rise in his support at the news that he had returned to the homeland—Dom Antonio, once installed as Portugal's king, would grant England a monopoly on the East Indies trade. The restoration would be a crushing blow to Philip, and Drake could use his forces to destroy the remainder of the Armada in its Iberian ports.

The invasion, which was launched in the spring of 1589, was a fiasco. Dom Antonio was put ashore in his homeland, and the English forces menaced Lisbon, but the Portuguese proved indifferent to the pretender's return, and illness ravaged Drake's fleet, leaving him unable to launch an attack on Spanish ports. A strange air of caution, a certain hesitancy, characterized his conduct of the campaign; he had been unwell immediately following the defeat of the Armada, and it seemed as if his bountiful store of energy was finally being exhausted.

Drake returned to England in disrepute, and his long-frustrated rivals at court seized the rare opportunity to discredit him. With England now secure from invasions, Elizabeth had little interest in ambitious naval strikes against Spanish interests and thus few projects for Drake, who retired to Plymouth and private life. During these years he was returned to Parliament, where his most notable achievements were arranging for the fortification of Plymouth and the construction of a 17-mile sluiceway that channeled fresh water from a countryside river to the city and its harbor. The project, completed under his supervision by April 1591 in less than six months, provided the city with water for the next 300 years. On the day the sluiceway was completed, Drake is said to have galloped along the still-dry course of the channel on horseback, racing the stream that followed him as cheering crowds welcomed him and the first rushing waters to Plymouth.

Several years passed in this fashion, with Drake occupying himself in Parliament with the sponsorship of bills concerning enterprises against Philip and in private with the accumulation of real estate, until at last, in 1595, the usual syndicate of the Crown and private business interests outfitted a grand expedition for the purpose of once more attacking Philip's holdings in the West Indies. Reunited at its helm, still vowing revenge for the disgrace they had known together 27 years before at San Juan de Ulúa, were Sir John Hawkins and Sir Francis Drake.

This 1590 drawing shows the course of the canal Drake was having built in order to bring fresh water to Plymouth. For years afterward, the denizens of Plymouth celebrated a holiday on the anniversary of the "bringing of the waters"; one of the highlights of the festivities was the toast raised by the officers of the city government "to the pious memory of Sir Francis Drake."

Though it was Drake's participation that had attracted
the majority of investors to the project, Elizabeth again felt
compelled to make him share leadership, for the same
reasons that she had placed Lord Howard above him in
countering the Armada. But, as Drake's biographer John
Sugden has pointed out, the divided command this time
was a "recipe for discord." Hawkins, who was now in his
sixties, was Drake's antithesis as a commander—slow, con-
servative, and wary—and he was less willing than Howard
had been to defer to his counterpart. The loyalties of the
2,500 men who manned the fleet's 27 ships were divided as
well, and dissension was evident even as the expedition was
preparing to depart. The delays that resulted allowed
Philip's colonies in the Caribbean to prepare for the
English onslaught, and Drake's provisioning of his ships was
hasty and haphazard. At sea, the two commanders quar-
reled constantly over tactics and Drake's insistence that the
unwilling Hawkins share supplies; a participant in the
voyage commented on the "many unkind speeches" that
the two exchanged.

And no longer was Drake's daring sufficient to overcome
all obstacles. At San Juan, on the island of Puerto Rico, the
Spanish were ready for him. Hawkins died before an assault
could even be launched—illness was already ravaging the
invaders—and the English were easily driven off. Rio de
la Hacha and Santa Marta proved vulnerable and were
burned to the ground, but elsewhere Spain had built up its
defenses since the days when El Draque, the master thief
of the unknown world, had wreaked such havoc in the
tropical outposts of the Caribbean. Now, Drake professed
not even to recognize the Spanish Main that he had once
threatened to make his own. When Thomas Maynarde, a
member of the expedition, attempted to query the once
impudent corsair about his tactics, "he answered me with
grief, protesting that he was as ignorant of the Indies as
myself, and that he never thought any place could be so
changed, as it were from a delicious and pleasant arbour

"There must be a beginning of any great matter, but the continuing unto the end until it be thoroughly finished yields the true glory," Drake wrote in 1587. This likeness was done by Nicholas Hilliard in 1581, shortly after the seafarer had completed his greatest maritime feat—the circumnavigation of the world.

into a waste and desert wilderness. . . . Since his coming out of England he never saw sail worth giving chase to."

The demoralized fleet made Nombre de Dios in late January 1596. The onetime treasure house of the world was now a pestilence-ridden hellhole, and the Spanish regarded it as no great loss when Drake and his men burned it to the ground; it was never rebuilt. Disease was now rampant among the English, and Drake himself was obviously and rapidly failing; he spent most of his time shut up in his cabin, felled by the ravages of fever and the "bloody flux" (dysentery). On the night of January 27, 1596, off Portobelo, Nombre de Dios's successor as Spain's most important Caribbean port on the isthmus, a delirious Drake rose from his sickbed and ordered an attendant to dress him in his war armor. He was dead before the dawn. In homage to his passing, his officers had Portobelo torched and two blazing fire ships set adrift during his funeral; hundreds of cannons boomed out a farewell salute as a lead-lined casket carried Drake's body to the bottom of the bay and the same waters where he had won his first victories closed over his final defeat.

Further Reading

Boorstin, Daniel J. *The Discoverers: A History of Man's Search to Know His World and Himself.* New York: Vintage, 1983.

Bradford, Ernle. *The Wind Commands Me, A Life of Sir Francis Drake.* New York: Harcourt Brace Jovanovich, 1965.

British Library Staff. *Sir Francis Drake.* Wolfeboro, NH: Longwood, 1977.

Cameron, Ian. *Lost Paradise, The Exploration of the Pacific.* Topsfield, MA: Salem House, 1987.

Corbett, Julian. *Sir Francis Drake.* New York: Haskell, 1969.

Corbett, Sir Julian. *For God and Gold.* London: N.p., 1894.

———. *Drake and the Tudor Navy.* 2 vols. London: Macmillan, 1898.

Dahlberg, Jacob, ed. *The Gold of Ophir: Travels, Myths and Legends in the New World.* New York: Dutton, 1972.

Debenham, Frank. *Discovery and Exploration: An Atlas History of Man's Wanderings.* Garden City, NY: Doubleday, 1960.

Drake, Sir Francis. *The World Encompassed by Sir Francis Drake.* New York: Harper & Row, 1977.

Hampden, John, ed. *Francis Drake, Privateer; Contemporary Narratives and Documents.* London: Eyre Methuen, 1972.

Hanna, Warren L. *Lost Harbor: The Controversy over Drake's California Anchorage.* Berkeley: University of California Press, 1979.

Makee, Alexander. *The Queen's Corsair: Drake's Journey of Circumnavigation.* Portland, OR: International Specialized Book Services, 1978.

Means, Philip Ainsworth. *The Spanish Main, Focus of Envy 1492–1700.* New York: Scribners, 1935.

Morison, Samuel Eliot. *The Great Explorers, The European Discovery of America.* Oxford: Oxford University Press, 1978.

Outhwaite, Leonard. *Unrolling the Map: The Story of Exploration.* New York: Reynal and Hitchcock, 1935.

Sugden, John. *Sir Francis Drake.* New York: Henry Holt, 1991.

Thomson, George Malcolm. *Sir Francis Drake.* New York: Morrow, 1972.

Walker, Bryce, ed. *The Armada.* New York: Time-Life Books, 1981.

Wood, W. Charles Henry. *Elizabethan Sea-Dogs, A Chronicle of Drake and His Companions.* New Haven: Yale University Press, 1918.

Chronology

1579	Captures Spanish treasure ship the *Nuestra Señora de la Concepción*; sails as far north as Vancouver Island; claims California territories for Elizabeth, first English "possession" in the New World; crosses Pacific to the Philippines; barters for rights to spice trade with sultan of Ternate
1580	Returns to England in completion of circumnavigation of the world; Spain annexes Portugal
1581–84	Drake knighted by Elizabeth; becomes mayor of Plymouth; buys Buckland Abbey; first wife dies; marries Elizabeth Sydenham, daughter of an aristocrat
1585–86	Conducts successful raids on the West Indies
1587	Raids Cádiz, Sagres, and the Algarve fisheries in order to "impeach the provisions of Spain" and hamper Philip II's plans to launch an armada against England
1588	Philip II launches the Spanish Armada against England; Drake, as vice admiral of English fleet, leads successful defense of the realm
1589	"Lisbon Expedition" to install Dom Antonio on Portuguese throne fails; Drake falls into disfavor
1590–95	Builds Plymouth watercourse; elected member of Parliament
1595–96	Leads unsuccessful raid on the Spanish Main in joint command with John Hawkins; both die at sea
1598	King Philip II of Spain dies
1603	Queen Elizabeth I dies
1604	Treaty of London is signed by England and Spain, temporarily ending hostilities between the two nations

Index

Picture Credits

Archivo General de Indias, Seville: p. 31; Art Resource, NY: p. 52; The Bettmann Archive: pp. 23, 58; Bettmann/Hulton: p. 33; Bridgeman Art Library/Art Resource, NY: pp. 74; The British Library (Photos from General Research Division, The New York Public Library, Astor, Lenox & Tilden Foundations): pp. 27 (Cotton MS, Augustin I.i, 38), 101 (Cotton MS, Augustin I.i, 41), 96 (Department of Manuscripts, Add MS. 33740, F.6), 24 (Map Division), 34 (Map Division), 66 (Map Division C.7.c.24, 1621 atlas with map in its first state), 83 (Map Division), 59 (Sloane MS, no.61), 65 (Sloane MS, no.61); The Hispanic Society of America, in *Atlas of Sea Charts* (K3): p. 37; Library of Congress: cover, pp. 20 (neg.# LCUSZ62–10214), 30 (neg.# LC–USZ62–38402), 43 (neg.# LC–USZ62–33896), 44 (neg.# LCUSZ62–68525), 50, 54, 60, 64 (neg.# LC–USZ62–71984), 72 (neg.# LC–USZ62–50791), 84; Master and Fellows, Magdalene College, Cambridge: p. 32; National Maritime Museum, London: pp. 14, 29, 48, 62 (Photo from General Research Division, The New York Public Library, Astor, Lenox & Tilden Foundations), 73, 78, 82 (Photo from General Research Division, The New York Public Library, Astor, Lenox & Tilden Foundations), 88, 90, 93, 97, 98, 99, 100; By Courtesy of the National Portrait Gallery, London: cover, pp. 12, 51, 75, 80, 103; Plymouth City Museums and Art Gallery Collections: pp. 17, 57, 86; Rare Books and Manuscripts Division, The New York Public Library, Astor, Lenox & Tilden Foundations: p. 40; *Queen Elizabeth, Defeat of the Spanish Armada*, St. Faith's Church, Gaylord, King's Lynn: p. 76; Scala/Art Resource, NY: pp. 21, 79; Society of Apothecaries of London: pp. 76–77

Alice Smith Duncan, former publications director for Bennington College, is the editor of *Publication Education Alert*, a journal for New York City educational reforms and school advocacy. Her interest in Drake was inspired by her grandfather, who ran away to sea at age 14 to be a cabin boy aboard a clipper ship bound for South America, worked his way up through the ranks of seaman, navigator, and commander during a distinguished 48-year naval career, and won the Navy Cross for heroism.

William H. Goetzmann holds the Jack S. Blanton, Sr., Chair in History at the University of Texas at Austin, where he has taught for many years. The author of numerous works on American history and exploration, he won the 1967 Pulitzer and Parkman prizes for his *Exploration and Empire: The Role of the Explorer and Scientist in the Winning of the American West, 1800–1900*. With his son William N. Goetzmann, he coauthored *The West of the Imagination*, which received the Carr P. Collins Award in 1986 from the Texas Institute of Letters. His documentary television series of the same name received a blue ribbon in the history category at the American Film and Video Festival held in New York City in 1987. A recent work, *New Lands, New Men: America and the Second Great Age of Discovery*, was published in 1986 to much critical acclaim.

Michael Collins served as command module pilot on the *Apollo 11* space mission, which landed his colleagues Neil Armstrong and Buzz Aldrin on the moon. A graduate of the United States Military Academy, Collins was named an astronaut in 1963. In 1966 he piloted the *Gemini 10* mission, during which he became the third American to walk in space. The author of several books on space exploration, Collins was director of the Smithsonian Institution's National Air and Space Museum from 1971 to 1978 and is a recipient of the Presidential Medal of Freedom.